The Spanish
Goalkeeping Bible

Laureano Ruiz

REEDSWAIN PUBLISHING

**Library of Congress
Cataloging - in - Publication Data**

by Laureano Ruiz
　　The Spanish Goalkeeping Bible

ISBN No. 1-59164-023-7
Lib. of Congress Catalog No. 2002107647
© 2002

*Translated at Bray's English
Centre, Santander by*
Jimmy Basterrechea and
Alan Bray

Editor
Bryan R. Beaver

Printed by
DATA REPRODUCTIONS
Auburn, Michigan

Reedswain Publishing
612 Pughtown Road
Spring City, PA 19475
800.331.5191
www.reedswain.com
info@reedswain.com

Contents

Foreword

I am 26 years of age and I have made it to the very top in the game: I play for Real Madrid and I am a full International with the Spanish team. My task now is to keep playing at this standard.

I am extremely proud of what I have achieved in the game especially as at first I had to overcome some tremendous set-backs (I spent 4 seasons on the subs bench at Racing de Santander – my home town). I think that under the same circumstances a lot of players would have thrown in the towel and given up. But not me, I worked hard and persevered. And when on occasion my head dropped there was Laureano to raise my spirits and to give me renewed impetus to continue (he was also there during the good times telling me to keep my feet on the ground and to continue working hard).

Laureano is a true 'maestro' of soccer. The majority of coaches choose tall and strong 14 year olds with the sole intention of winning games (which they often lose) without giving them a proper grounding in the game. I am short (1.67m) and so I would never have even been given a chance under these coaches. But Laureano is different. He is more concerned with teaching the players to use the ball effectively, pass and make space, pace themselves throughout the game, develop fighting spirit and strong will-power, and above all, participate and be creative. He achieves this by giving good advice, clear instructions and thanks to his vast knowledge and experience in the game and his practical demonstrations.

The majority of coaches merely regurgitate what was drilled in to them 15-20 years ago by their coach. But the routines, the knowledge and the drills are all outdated as they are merely handed down from coach to coach over the years. It is a vicious circle. However, Laureano does not follow this pattern. He is at the cutting edge of soccer training, making full use of all his knowledge and experience in the game to help train players to meet the needs of the modern game.

Thanks to his extensive experience as a coach (at 18 he played for Racing de Santander and was coaching the youth team) many players have played in the Spanish First Division and as full internationals: Aguilar, Santillana, Juan Carlos, Chinchón, Olmo, Sánchez, Carrasco, Caldere, Rojo, Moratalla, Quique Setien (present coach of Racing de Santander), Ferrer, Luis and Ivan Helguera, De la Peña and many more including myself.

He has coached some of the top players in the game: the Spanish players Migueli, Marciál and Rexach (currently coach of Footbal Club Barcelona), the Dutch players Neeskens and the legendary Cruyff, the Argentine Heredia, the Peruvian Sotil and the Portuguese goalkeeper Damas and they have all commented on different occasions that: "The best coach I have had was Laureano Ruiz." In other words, he is the best coach around.

I always looked on with interest and listened attentively as he gave advice to the goalkeepers as this greatly helped my game as an attacker. For example, when he says "The goalkeeper is the first attacker" I make sure that I run alongside the opponent's goalkeeper when he has got the ball in order to allow my team-mates more time to reorganize and get in position. When he says "The closer you get to goal the further you are from scoring" I make sure that I shoot as quickly as possible before the goal-keeper has a chance to run out and narrow the angle.

This wonderful book is full of lots of other tips and sugges-tions that will help goalkeepers, outfield players and coaches improve their performance.

Let me finish by expressing my gratitude to Laureano and by thoroughly recommending this book which is full of practical and useful advice for everyone who is passionate about this wonder-ful game.

Thanks 'maestro'

Pedro Munitis Álvarez

The History of the Goalkeeper

The modern game of soccer can be traced back to the Freemasons' Tavern in London, where, on 26th October 1863, the representatives of eleven clubs met to establish what would later become the most important Association in the world.

In those early days there was no limit on the number of players per team. Players could control the ball and run with it using their hands, just as in the game of rugby, and the goalmouth consisted of two posts with no crossbar. To score a goal the ball had to be passed at any height between these two posts. Under these rules a goalkeeper was not necessary, as any player could stop a goal being scored by using his body, feet or hands. It is interesting to note that goalkeepers were not even discussed at that initial meeting in the Freemasons' Tavern.

This depicts an early game of soccer played in London in 1891. For the first time, the goals had crossbars and nets. There is also a 'goal judge'(on the left) holding a flag. This position evolved into the referee's assistant (formerly known as the linesman).

From 1870 all players were prohibited from touching the ball with their arms or hands. This provoked widespread condemnation. So much so that the rule was subsequently changed so that one player per team was able to touch the ball with his hands, but only in his own half of the pitch. This player also had to dress differently from his teammates and the opposition so that he could be easily recognized. In 1871 some clubs, unhappy with these rule changes, broke away from the Association to form the Rugby Football Union. Later, the rule was changed again so that this one player could only touch the ball with his hands in his own penalty area. This rule continues today. Thus the goalkeeper, a unique player, was born. It is the most recent position created in the game and yet this position has undergone more tactical and technical changes than any other and the goalkeeper has developed into the most complete player in the sport.

When this 'different' player was first introduced into the game he did not stay on the goal-line between the goalposts. Because there was no crossbar, he could do little from this position.

Instead he was able to play anywhere on the pitch using both his feet and especially his hands to great advantage. Years later the rule was changed again, stating that this player could only use his hands near his own goalmouth area, but he was still free to play all over the pitch.

Finally, the goalmouth was given the dimensions that are still used today - crossbar 8 yards, posts 8 feet. Nevertheless, the goalkeeper was still not required to stay near the goal because if there was a possibility of a goal being scored any player could stop the attack by any means necessary, not worrying about causing a serious foul because the penalty kick had not yet been introduced. A free kick was awarded but all the defenders stood on the goal-line and goals rarely resulted.

In 1890 the Everton goalkeeper William McCrum suggested that penalty kicks should be awarded for any foul in the goalkeeper's area. On 2nd June 1891 the International Board decided that goalkeepers would have to remain in their area and that penalty kicks would be introduced into the game. Until this time all goalkeepers were rather big and clumsy and they used any means necessary to stop their opponent from scoring. However, once these new rule changes came into force the physical characteristics of the goalkeeper changed significantly. The traditional big stocky goalkeepers did not have the mobility to make saves and stop low shots. The new breed of goalkeeper was just as brave, between 5'10" and 6' 1", but far more athletic.

The evolution of the "different" player

Over the last 40-50 years the rules and tactics of soccer have changed significantly. Naturally enough, goalkeepers have also been affected by these changes. One of these tactics was called the 'pyramid' system. The 'pyramid' system was a tactic used by the defense which left the goalkeeper very little to do as he was protected by the 'offside' rule. The 'offside' rule today states that a free kick will be awarded if the ball is passed to a player when there are less than a minimum of two opposing players (one being the goalkeeper) between him and the goal. In the early days three players in the opposition had to be between the striker and the goal. All players were penalized whether or not they were interfering with play. Thankfully this law has been changed and now 'offside' is only given if the player is interfering with play or seeking to gain an unfair advantage from his position. In those early days a player could also be given 'offside' from a throw-in, but this rule was also changed during the same period. After these rule changes, the two defenders and the goalkeeper were left powerless to prevent lots of goals being scored because they were not used to working hard. The W-M system was introduced to combat this problem. This formation used 3 defenders which gave the goalkeeper greater protection. However, as part of the system, the goalkeeper was now expected to rush off his line to repel any possible threat on goal. This new breed of goalkeeper needed to be fast, agile, a good shot stopper and safe with his fists.

Even with the arrival of the "back four", 4-4-2 and 4-3-3, the goalkeeper was still expected to intercept and cut-out balls where appropriate. The Hungarian goalkeeper Grocics took this one step further and on several occasions during a match he often played outside his area, almost acting as an extra defender. The Russian goalkeeper Yashin was also renowned for doing this from time to time.

In 1967, after the World Cup in England, a rule was introduced that would have a significant impact on goalkeepers. Up to this time the goalkeeper was able to keep possession of the ball indefinitely as long as he kept bouncing it. If his team was winning with a few minutes to go then the goalkeeper would waste time by keeping possession of the ball until he was invariably fouled by a frustrated attacker. A free-kick was awarded and the time-wasting would begin again. To get over this problem the International Board introduced the 4 step or 4 second rule. This rule stated that the goalkeeper had to release the ball quickly and that he could not be impeded from doing so by the opposition or else a free-kick would be awarded. This new law highlighted something that I had been thinking for some time. The new law proved that the best time for the goalkeeper to release the ball is immediately after the opposition loses possession because at this precise moment they are all out of position. This new rule had a significant impact on the game because now, for the first time, the goalkeeper could influence the attack. Consequently the goalkeeper was forced to be more of a soccer player. Among other things, he needed the ability to be able to pass or throw the ball out quickly to a specific teammate. Today, the goalkeeper is an integral part of many swift and decisive counter-attacks. During Euro-96 the Dutch goalkeeper Van Der Sar, received the ball and released it as quickly as possible, enabling his teammate Bergkamp to go on and score a brilliant goal.

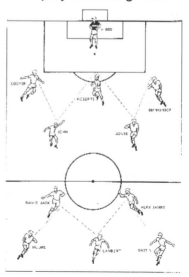

The W-M system played by the English team Arsenal.

With the introduction of the 'sweeper', the goalkeeper spent most of his time on or near his own goal-line and rarely strayed from this position. He also became more instrumental in organizing the defense by shouting clear brief instructions or via a series of expressions and signals. In this way, a deep understanding developed between the goalkeeper and the rest of his teammates as they appreciated his tactical knowledge and soccer brain.

The Dutch goalkeeper Van Der Sar is a 'complete' goalkeeper.

Nowadays, soccer is played at a much faster pace and this is largely due to the more efficient and appropriate training techniques. The tendency for teams to 'push up' more, use the 'offside' rule and play the 'pressing' game means that the role of the goalkeeper is more important than ever. Not only does he have to perform well in goal but he also has to play off his goal-line and even outside the 18-yard box while at the same time not forgetting to shout advice and instructions to his teammates.

Nevertheless, it is important for the team to fully understand whether the system involves using the goalkeeper as above or whether a 'sweeper' is used instead. If the 'sweeper' is used then the goalkeeper is far less involved in the collective play as he stays near his goal while the former organizes the team and initiates the attacking moves. It is an exaggeration to suggest that the goalkeeper stands 'glued' to his goal-line but under the 'sweeper' system he will certainly not play like Molina (the Deportivo goalkeeper) did when he was at Athletico Madrid, as his defenders played 'flat' near the half way line, leaving him to cover all the space behind them. The role of the goalkeeper, therefore, largely depends on the system of play e.g. at Barcelona the goalkeeper played completely differently under Robson compared to when Cruyff was in charge.

However, regardless of what the system is, the important thing is that the goalkeeper knows it, fully understands it and helps to transmit it to his teammates. I should point out that when I refer to 'the method' I make little specific reference to the role of the goalkeeper. This is because it seems only obvious that they should be present and involved in all of the theoretical and practical training when learning the system of play and the game plan. The coach needs to make sure that the goalkeeper knows what advice and instructions he needs to shout to his teammates. Unbelievable as it may seem, some coaches completely segregate the goalkeeper from the rest of his teammates during both the theoretical and the practical training sessions (I will go into this in more detail later in the book).

If the goalkeepers are not involved in all the training sessions and only attend the general planning session, then it is no surprise that they are left speechless and clueless when asked any question on the subject because they just do not know what is expected of them or how the team is going to play. Unfortunately, even if the coach outlines the system and game plan to a reasonably experienced goalkeeper there is a strong possibility that he may not understand it. This is because he has spent so many years only concentrating on shot-stopping etc and has never been included in the collective team training.

Not only does the goalkeeper need to fully understand the system of play but he also needs to know the strengths and weaknesses of his teammates (especially the defenders). This is so he is given no surprises during the match and also helps him to gauge when to shout out instructions and advise as he sees potentially dangerous moves develop. The goalkeeper also needs to be aware of how his defenders are likely to fair against the players they are marking.

For the same reasons, the goalkeeper needs to know the quality of the opposition (especially the attackers):

- *Favorite techniques and moves: heading ability, dribbling skill, long range shots etc.*

- *Preferred foot (right-footed, left-footed or two-footed), good in the air, accurate passer, powerful shot.*

- *Preferred moves: the 'one-two', switching the direction of play, how he makes space, unpredictable passes, crosses on the run etc.*

Of course, it is true that these days coaches are able to study each individual player in great detail on video or computer and so the players with a small technical repertoire offer few problems or surprises. The goalkeeper is also fully prepared for the 'dead ball' specialist as he is able to study his preferred techniques from: free kicks and corners, unpredictable shots and especially penalties. Nevertheless, at the time the penalty is about to be taken both players suffer a host of mixed emotions. Both the goalkeeper and the penalty taker know that the other has studied what he is likely to do in this situation and so a war of nerves takes place which has a less than certain outcome. This intense period of mental stress was summed up perfectly by the Italian goalkeeper Zenga, when he wrote in the 'Gazzetta Dello Sport', "I know that you know what I know, just as you know that I know what you know."

FIFA Decides to Make Changes

After the disappointing World Cup in Italy, FIFA decided to make some rule changes in order to make the game more offensive and more entertaining. Without doubt, the most important rule-change was the abolition of the back pass to the goalkeeper. This rule had already been introduced with great success into other sports such as handball. I think the rule should go further, banning the back pass altogether, regardless of what part of the body is used, including the head or chest. This rule change meant that the defense could no longer take the easy way out and pass back to the goalkeeper when under pressure from the opposition's attack. A team would waste time, if they were winning, by repeatedly passing back to the goalkeeper, often leaving the opposition disillusioned and powerless to respond. The end result was always that the game died a slow death and was very unentertaining to watch. Now that the back pass to the goalkeeper has been abolished, the losing team can at least mount attacks and even score during the final moments of a game. On other occasions the losing team attack so much that they leave themselves vulnerable at the back and the team winning has no choice but to mount a counter-attack when they get the possibility (to relieve the pressure if nothing else) and they create chances or even increase their lead.

All this has created a far more attacking and entertaining game and at the same time made the goalkeeper's role a lot more difficult and complicated. However, playing in goal is and always will be a challenge for the majority of players as the philosophy, ideas and movements are not the same as for outfield players.

Any goalkeeper who cannot use his feet can get himself into all sorts of difficulties (I remember the calamitous pass Zubizarreta made to Laudrup which almost knocked Spain out of the '94 World Cup) which often lead to unnecessary goals being scored. By contrast, any goalkeeper who is able to use his feet to good effect has a tremendous advantage. I am convinced that thanks to this ability, Busquets played in goal for Barça and Prats was picked to play for Betis. Their foot skills were the envy of many outfield players.

This rule change meant that a new breed of goalkeeper was needed in the game. The next generation of goalkeepers will not have to adapt to the new situation as they will be well accustomed to it.

These are the attributes a goalkeeper should have:

1. He should not be particularly short or exceptionally tall. As a general rule goalkeepers are usually between 5' 10" and 6' 1". If the goalkeeper is any shorter than this, he will find it difficult to reach the balls placed near the top corner of the goal and he will also find it difficult to compete for the high balls and crosses with the opposition. If a goalkeeper is too tall then usually he will find it difficult to get down quickly to reach the low shots. Tall goalkeepers are usually less agile and react more slowly than average size players.

2. A minimum height is a pre-requisite but this is of little consequence if the goalkeeper does not also have the following physical characteristics: a good reach, big hands (with a good feel for the ball) and an overall good physique and physical fitness.

3. His weight should be in proportion to his height and the goal keeper should have the necessary physical strength which allows him to take powerfully struck goal kicks and challenge effectively for high balls and crosses with the opposition.

4. Quick reflexes. Often the outcome of an intervention depends on a tenth of a second and so good reaction speed is essential.

5. Great flexibility and elasticity. Stiff and rigid musculature and joints are not compatible with the wide range of movements the goalkeeper has to make.

6. Goalkeepers are also usually fast runners. Some people (including some goalkeepers) think that this is not necessary, but imagine the situation as an attack breaks down and the opposition mounts a swift counterattack. A fast goalkeeper is able to run off his line to intercept the ball and end the danger. Also, any team that plays the 'offside' trap needs a fast goalkeeper to act as the last defender to cut out long balls, often from outside the 18-yard box. Even under normal circumstances a split second is sometimes the only difference between success and failure when trying to get back into position or narrow the angle.

Even if the goalkeeper has all these attributes and physical qualities he will never be a great goalkeeper unless these are complimented by the following psychological considerations:

a) The goalkeeper needs to stay calm and be patient. He needs to keep calm in order to analyze and think quickly no matter what the situation so that he has more chance of coming up with the right solution. He needs to be patient and not let a lack of concentration or a bad mistake upset his game. If he loses control and his head drops, more mistakes and goals will surely follow.

b) The goalkeeper must be able to multi-task (concentrate on more than one thing at a time). He needs to observe everything that happens on the pitch: the movements of the opposition, teammates and the ball. He also needs to anticipate how a move is likely to develop in order to shout the appropriate instructions to his defenders or intervene himself where necessary.

c) Another tremendous asset for the goalkeeper and perhaps the most important is good positioning sense. Some goalkeepers seem to attract the ball. They do not need to make many spectacular diving saves because thanks to their anticipation and positioning they are always in the right place at the right time and therefore hardly need to move at all. This is not an easy skill to acquire as it necessitates a thorough knowledge of the individual players in the opposition and of the game of soccer itself. Of course, apart from a few exceptions, there is no substitute for experience and so for most players this quality improves over the years.

Are only experienced goalkeepers good?

The most important thing to get right in training is the mind. It is a pre-requisite for any goalkeeper to have tremendous concentration and motivation to play in the modern game. The days when the goalkeeper could chat with supporters (or exchange insults with rival fans) have long since disappeared. Now, not only is the emphasis on total concentration throughout the whole match but also the goalkeeper has to occupy his mind with a number of different things all at once. His mindset needs to be resilient enough to cope with the wide range of emotions that could (if concentration wavers) affect his game. An elementary mistake one minute that leads to a goal may be followed by a dramatic match-winning penalty save the next.

The majority of coaches believe that a player will automatically become a top goalkeeper after lots of experience and many years in the game. There is even a well-known saying in the game: "You have to be between 28-30 years old to be a great goalkeeper". Of course it is true (not in all cases) that the player's age has a direct affect on his mental maturity and that very few young players have this gift. But I do not understand why there is such disparity between the general age of a top outfield player and that of a top goalkeeper. A goalkeeper has to be a 'veteran', whereas an outfield player can reach the top of the game when he is 18-20.

My own personal opinion, which I am passionate about, I will try to explain in the following two points:

1. When the majority of coaches see a player wearing the number '1' shirt they believe in him totally and they give him what they think is the very best training program: meticulous and constant attention working on technique, physical fitness, psychological pointers, advising and coaching him to become familiar with all the different moves and situations he is likely to face in a game. Finally, most importantly, he gets what every player needs, an opportunity to play.

2. However, there needs to be a far greater emphasis on psychology where young goalkeepers are concerned because they have a tremendous responsibility on their shoulders. The goalkeeper knows that any mistake he makes may prove crucial to the outcome of the game. Any error he makes, however simple, is rarely of little consequence. This is why he needs support and confidence-building advice from the coach in order to slowly but surely gain experience and iron-out any slight weaknesses in his game. Unfortunately, very few coaches are patient with young goalkeepers. They do not give them the necessary physical, technical or psychological training and they make little effort to try to really understand the work and needs of the goalkeeper. In reality, the goalkeeper is often not coached at all. Instead he is made to train on his own, on an individual basis, which has little to do with the movements and thought processes made in a real game. Add to this the fact that good young goalkeepers are snapped up quickly by the top teams who rout the opposition every week, and so they act as mere spectators cheering every goal from the other end of the pitch.

Gianluigi Buffon

I have already said that a goalkeeper can reach the top of the game at a very young age and that he does not have to wait until he is 28-30 years old. A good example of this is the Italian Gianluigi Buffón, nephew of the legendary Lorenzo Buffón, the ex-Milan and Italian international goalkeeper.

Gianluigi was born on 28th January 1978 and he has already played at every international level (sub-15, sub-17, sub-18, sub-21 and the full national team itself). He started playing in goal for Serie 'A' team Parma when he was only 16 years old. He spent the 94-95 season as a reserve goalkeeper for the national team, learning from the veteran goalkeeper Bucci (who was first-team choice) and Nesta. The following season Bucci got injured the day before the clash with the then all-powerful Milan. The coach, Nervio Scala, decided to play Buffón. The game finished goal-less, thanks largely to the brilliance of the young 17 year old goalkeeper.

Since that day he kept his place in the first-team and the great Bucci was transferred to another club. Buffón has performed so well that Césare Maldini (who picked him to play at sub-21 level) has selected him for the international squad. The first-choice goalkeeper, Pagliuici got injured during the decisive qualification match against Russia for France '98. Up stepped Buffón onto the snow-covered pitch and against a rival determined to make his international debut a baptism of fire. The 19 year old sailed through his first match with an outstanding performance.

His greatest strengths are: excellent organization and positioning of teammates, he dominates his area and he never loses his nerve. His own positioning is excellent and he is a master at '1 v 1' with a striker. He also has a tremendous instinct for saving penalties as he has saved many both for Parma and the national team (in recent years he also saved two penalties taken by Andreas Moller for Borussia in one match against much to the despair of his ex-coach Nevio Scala).

In other words, despite being very young he already has all the necessary qualities that make a top goalkeeper. He now plays for Juventus.

This of course is a great set back to the talented goalkeeper as far as development and progression is concerned. Either way, the coach will not give him all the attention he requires in training because he is in the first-team and therefore gets a game every week. Ironically, an outstanding reserve goalkeeper who rarely plays in the team has more chance of better training and an improved developmental trajectory.

GOALKEEPER TO PLAYER

As I have already mentioned, the new rule changes meant that new skills and techniques became fundamental for the goalkeeper in the modern game. I am referring in particular to ball control, knowledge and understanding of the game.

As far as ball control is concerned, we can all appreciate if a goalkeeper is good or bad at resolving difficult situations using his feet in and beyond the 18-yard box. However, not all goalkeepers are so sure about how to 'read' the game and what this involves. They do not know how to deal with the numerous and varied situations that occur during a game. There is no doubt that of all the different things a goalkeeper has to worry about this is by far the most difficult. A player can be tremendously fit with great technique but have little idea how to play the game.

This is also true of goalkeepers. Qualities such as intelligence, perceptiveness and a 'real' understanding of the game facilitate a keen sense of anticipation, but few spectators are able to understand or appreciate this. Unfortunately, this is also a mystery for many coaches in the game. This is why goalkeepers are chosen for being tall and strong. The coach does not notice all the other qualities and some even say: "I can't judge how good he is if he hasn't had a shot to save." Yes, the opposition has not had a shot, but this was due to the goalkeeper's ability to organize his defenders and his great sense of anticipation. This is a difficult concept for young goalkeepers to understand as well. They always want to intervene and see as much of the ball as possible as they think this is the only way to stand out and make an impression. Unfortunately, any goalkeeper who continues to think this way will have a very limited future in the game.

It is true to say that the goalkeeper has the most multi-tasking role in the game: he has to play well in goal, he has to deal with situations off his line (often beyond the 18-yard box), he has to have good ball control so that he can dribble his way out of trouble or pass to a teammate, and most importantly, because of the complexity of the modern game he has to organize his defense while at the same time anticipate when they are likely to make a mistake so that he can intervene himself to help prevent a clear chance on goal. If the goalkeeper understands this role and can 'read' the game then he is helped by the fact that he can see all the play developing in front of him.

Taking all of the above qualities into account, the goalkeeper of tomorrow needs to be even more of a complete player. The goalkeeper will need to have the same tactical awareness as the outfield players, not only to deal with balls passed to him by a teammate but also to get involved in starting the offensive moves. A hint of what the goalkeepers of the future might be like can be seen today by watching three Latin American goalkeepers. They place far more emphasis on technical, tactical training and all-round soccer ability in these countries. The specific goalkeepers I am referring to are Chilavert from Paraguay, Higuita from Colombia and Campos from Mexico.

The ex-Valladolid player, Higuita, has amazing technical ability and even when playing in goal he was able to produce breathtaking silky skills, incredible passes and even decisive goals. Perhaps the most fresh in the memory is the night he thrilled the Wembley crowd during a recent England vs Columbia match: the English tried a long shot but Higuita, instead of being content with merely blocking or catching the ball decided to move forward Chilean-style (what some people call the 'scorpion') as if going to do a handstand and sent the ball back in the same direction with his heels. The coach and some of his own teammates almost had a heart-attack.

The Mexican Campos is another player who is not just a goalkeeper but is also a great all round soccer player. He is known throughout the world for his multi-colored kit. Campos alternates his position, playing in goal one match and then as a creative outfield player in the next. In June 1996, he played 2 matches in 4 hours. The first was for Mexico vs USA in the Rose bowl, Pasadena. Then in the same stadium, he also played in goal for his club team Galaxy against Tampa Bay in an MLS match. With 20 minutes to go and with his side losing 2-1, Campos changed out of his multi-colored kit to play as an attacker. Campos was the stimulus his side needed. Playing inspired soccer, he was able to score the equalizer.

Without doubt, the Paraguayan Chilavert is the archetypal complete player. Over the last few years, Chilavert, who played for Zaragoza between 1988-1991, has developed into a goal scoring machine. Not only that, but his goals tend to be brilliant and decisive. He is able to score from anywhere, including free-kicks, penalties, long range shots and thanks to his prodigious leap, from corners. In March 1996, he scored 2 goals against Maradona's Boca Juniors. The first was a powerfully struck free-kick which almost broke the back of the net and the second goal was scored from a penalty. In June of the same year, he scored one of the most incredible goals in the history of the game. Much to the astonishment of the crowd, he sent the ball rocketing into the River Plate net from 60 yards. The only person not surprised by the strike was perhaps Chilavert himself as he was used to scoring breathtaking goals. Similar goals have also been scored by Campos while playing in a friendly international and by the irrepressible Higuita while playing in the Copa de la Libertadores. But it is difficult to outdo Chilavert. In September 1996, during a World Cup '98 qualifying match between Argentina and Paraguay, he scored with a blistering free-kick to level the match. Then later, in the same match, when Batistuta was convinced he was about to score the winner, Chilavert somehow managed to push the shot for a corner with the tips of his fingers. At the end of the match, the idiosyncratic Paraguayan was carried shoulder high by his teammates and some of the fans.

It is no surprise that the charismatic 'Lord Paragua' should reach the pinnacle of his illustrious career as a goalkeeper/for-ward in 1996 when he was named the best soccer player in the Americas by the Uruguayan newspaper 'El Pais'. This was a first, as the award had never gone to a goalkeeper. In the past the honor had always gone to legendary outfield players such as Pelé, Francescoli, Cubillas, Zíco, Kempes, Sócrates and Maradona.

With these goalkeepers the prophecy of Schoen the ex-West German manager was coming true. In 1972 he said, "There will come a day when the goalkeeper will play a key role as an extra attacker, instigating moves that result in goals. Do not think I am exaggerating when I suggest that in the future this will be an important tactic."

DIFFERENT OBJECTIVES AND TRAINING

During a match, the goalkeeper and his teammates have different roles to perform but their aims coincide. This is also true during training where different disciplines are required but the majority of the skills are largely the same. However, in reality, the training experienced by many goalkeepers lacks intensity and quality. It has very little to do with what a goalkeeper might be expected to do doing a match. To clarify this point let us look at the way goalkeepers have been coached over the years.

In the early days, goalkeepers and outfield players were trained in exactly the same way. The goalkeeper only practiced his specific role during matches. Later, the training routines became more diverse and more sophisticated.

a) *The goalkeeper joined in the general training sessions with the outfield players.*

b) *The goalkeeper would often stand in goal while the outfield players had shooting and crossing practice.*

c) *Sometimes, at the end of the training session the coach would have the goalkeeper save shots repeatedly.*

With few variations we have arrived at the present day situation. In recent years, some clubs have introduced a specific goalkeeping coach but the majority of clubs ignore the goalkeeper, leaving him to his own devices. Meanwhile the coach dedicates his time to the outfield players and thinks that any time spent with the goalkeeper is better served monitoring the development and progress of the outfield players. Clubs who have a goalkeeping coach train their goalkeepers in isolation. This seems totally incomprehensible as all the players form the same team and they all have the same aims.

Throughout the history the game, the technical and tactical role of the goalkeeper has always been divided into 5 different responsibilities: 4 defensive and 1 offensive.

Defensive:

1. How he performs as a shot stopper.

2. How he deals with dead-ball situations: corners penalties and free-kicks.

3. His ability to cope with the long through ball and crosses.

4. How he organizes his defenders and if he has the necessary anticipation in order to do this more effectively.

Offensive:

1. How he plays during the game using the same criteria as for an outfield player.

A goalkeeper with good ball skills was only common during the early days of soccer. Banning a goalkeeper from using his hands on a back pass from his teammates has had a big impact on his traditional role. This change has had a profound affect on goalkeepers at every level of the game (relative to age and standard).

This has been the impact of the change:

1. Until recently few people would have dared suggest that a goal keeper's attacking role was as important as his defensive duties. Of course it is true to say that the principal aim of a goalkeeper is to keep a clean sheet. However, nowadays the role of the goalkeeper has changed and he is expected to be equally comfortable in goal and anywhere on the pitch. There are many occasions throughout a game when a goalkeeper has to intervene with his feet or with his head, either to prevent a goal or start an attack.

2. Years ago, a disorganized defense could relieve the pressure and get out of trouble by passing back to the goalkeeper. This is not possible now. A goalkeeper needs to be much more alert in order to organize his defenders or intervene himself inside or outside his area. This total concentration is also needed to intercept a defense-splitting pass or to claim potentially dangerous crosses.

3. The ability to focus totally on the action is a big help in developing an acute sense of timing. The ability to judge the distance of the opposition and the speed and direction of the ball is an invaluable tool when deciding, in an instant, whether to go for the ball or not. Of course, this is very difficult for a goal keeper to learn quickly as it nearly always comes with experience. I have witnessed many mediocre goalkeepers or even outstanding apprentices misjudge a situation by failing to intervene and a goal is scored as a result. I point out the error and then watch the goalkeeper rush off his line to intercept the next attack. The goalkeeper has again totally misjudged the situation and he looks on in horror as the striker, fully in control of the ball, takes it past him. On other occasions he rushes off his line only to find that the defender gets to the ball first. If this happens the coach should not criticize the goalkeeper for coming off his line. The coach will soon find out from experience that if he does the goalkeeper will start to think, "I can't win, if I come off my line he tells me to stay put, if I stay put he tells me to run out. He's got a screw loose and he's driving me crazy." Instead, wait for the next training session and repeat these moves time after time.

4. Following on from the previous point, the ability to focus and totally concentrate is a tremendous attribute for any soccer player. It helps his creativity and his ability to follow the play.

However, such admirable qualities are of little use unless the player has a 'soccer brain'. A great goalkeeper with real 'vision' is able to anticipate both the likely actions of the opposition and those of his own players. He is able to predict the possible outcome of every situation and react accordingly. He rarely makes dramatic diving saves as he anticipates where each cross or shot is likely to go and gets into position.

5. Some coaches make their goalkeepers train in isolation. These players rarely practice real match situations and so often make errors of judgment during games. However, if the coach positions himself near the goalkeeper during a match then the goalkeeper's ability to make correct decisions seems to improve dramatically. This of course is because the coach is constantly telling him what to do. During the next game the goalkeeper continues to make errors as he can no longer hear the coach and he is unable to 'read' the game. Unfortunately, he never gets a chance to improve his positioning or timing because he is unable to practice these invaluable techniques during training. A goalkeeper needs to practice these situations time after time in order to acquire this skill. When should he come off his line? When should he come for a cross? The goalkeeper can only get a real feel and understanding for these situations by repeatedly practicing them on the training ground. After a while the goalkeeper will know when to come and his timing and judgment will improve dramatically.

6. As defenders can no longer pass back to the arms of the goalkeeper they often give away corners, free-kicks or even penalties. This inevitably means that more goal-scoring chances and goals result.

7. As already mentioned, this change means that the goalkeeper had far less pure goalkeeping duties to perform during a game. On average a goalkeeper touches the ball 27 times during a match; 14-16 of these are with his feet. By contrast, the goalkeeper makes far fewer diving saves. In 1970, a goalkeeper was likely to make 10-12 diving saves on average during a match. Today, the average number of dives during a game is 2-3. The goalkeeper is more likely to stretch for crosses or react in anticipation to a threat on goal.

8. The reality of the situation caused by this change to the back pass law is that a goalkeeper generally has less to do during a match. Before the rule change a goalkeeper would make 41 interventions on average during a match. After the back pass was banned the average number of interventions dropped to 27. As far as possession of the ball is concerned, this dropped from an average of 2 minutes 47 seconds per match to a miserly 46 seconds. It seems like a contradiction to suggest that more goal-scoring chances resulted after the rule change and yet the goalkeeper now sees less of the ball. But there is a simple explanation for this: before the rule change the goal-keeper became more involved in the game via the back pass and he wasted lots of time keeping possession of the ball.

9. A goalkeeper generally touches the ball 27 times during a match. This means he touches the ball every 3 minutes and 33 seconds. But it goes without saying that he may have busy periods when he touches the ball more often and long spells when he is not involved in the game. I have analyzed the different types of interventions and I think some coaches may find the results surprising:

a) 66% Back passes (gathering easy balls, goal kicks and inter-cepting long through balls).
b) 7% Gathering the ball at low, medium or high height.
c) 14% Rushing off line to catch or smother, either jumping or diving.
d) 9% Stretching or diving to save a certain goal.
e) 4% Deflecting shots wide of goal and the use of fists.

10. It is important to point out that a goalkeeper will have a lot more to do in a game if he plays for a weak or defensive team. The opposite is also true: if he plays in a powerful team, he is likely to be less involved in the match. Furthermore, playing for a strong team may disadvantage his progress as a goalkeeper. The long periods of inactivity will test his powers of concentration and he will not stay in tip-top shape. There is also the danger that if the opposition manage to mount an attack, the goalkeeper could be caught cold. On the other hand, even if the majority of his interventions are straightforward, the goalkeeper who plays in a weak team is always fully focused and warmed up. This activity breeds confidence and helps the goalkeeper deal more effectively with the dangerous situations when they arise. For this reason it makes sense that when a goalkeeper moves from a mediocre team to a strong one, and has little to do, the fans wonder what the coach ever saw in him.

11. Continuing the theme of the 27 interventions per match (which we know could obviously be more or less), when we watch Rossi, the Milan goalkeeper and other outstanding goalkeepers, we notice that they spend most of their time in or near their six yard box. Even when confronted with high balls or long passes into the 18 yard box, he remains unperturbed and stands his ground between the posts. His defenders deal with the majority of these balls and Rossi is left to demonstrate his ability only when there is a direct threat on goal. It is no surprise that Capello, after watching the two international goalkeepers, Buyo and Calizares, who are very keen on intervention, decided to sign Illgner who has a similar style to Rossi.

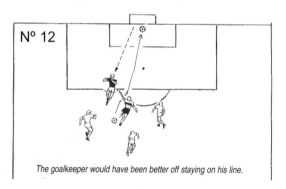

The goalkeeper would have been better off staying on his line.

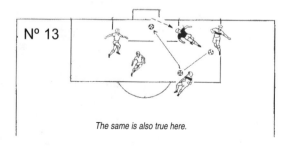

The same is also true here.

12. The truth is that most goalkeepers are obsessed with becoming directly involved in the game as this is where they hope to shine and impress. This is perhaps why they are so bad at reading the game (not all goalkeepers are so impulsive) and often misjudge the situation when trying to claim the ball. There is a saying that goalkeepers have always followed which is still true today, "Do not leave your goalmouth unless your defense has been beaten". We often see an attacker get clear of the defense but the defenders catch him just as he reaches the goal area, so he decides to shoot. However, he still manages to score even though he is tired and can only manage a weak shot. Why? Because the goalkeeper had rushed off his line to intercept the attacker and...

13. Another saying for goalkeepers: "If an attacker breaks free down the wing heading for the corner flag, do not try to claim the ball, never go beyond the far post. Wait". However, the goalkeeper with little knowledge of the game, who is anxious to intervene and has been told by his coach that he needs to close down his opponent and narrow the angle, cannot see that under these circumstances this is not appropriate and heads out towards the attacker. If the player in possession looks up and cuts the ball back towards the penalty spot, he invariably finds an open goal and an easy tap-in for a teammate.

14. It is well known that when the defense push up onto the halfway line the goalkeeper also plays further up the pitch, some times beyond his area. That said, our advice is never leave the 6-yard box if the pitch is muddy and soggy. Under these circumstances, if the goalkeeper decides to intervene, he could easily mistime his run if the ball gets held up in the mud. This could cause all sorts of problems. Also, if a player manages to get beyond the defense, then the soggy pitch could delay him long enough for the defenders to get back and make a challenge.

During the match between Rayo Vallecano and Sporting de Gijon on 27th January 1997, it was both amusing and pitiful to watch an experienced goalkeeper such as Ablanedo, continually misjudge his interventions as the ball kept getting stuck in the mud. If he had stayed in his goal, he would have left it to the attacker to overcome the difficulties presented by the muddy pitch.

15. Another move which is very common: an attacker breaks clear from the half way line, leaving the defenders in his wake. The panic-stricken goalkeeper rushes out, desperate to claim the ball. Until recently this would have been the correct decision because the goalkeeper was able to prevent a goal being scored by hand balling outside his area or by subtly fouling the attacker, resulting in a mere free kick. However, if a goalkeeper does this today, he is sent off for deliberate hand ball or for producing what is called a 'professional foul'. For this reason, nowadays the best tactic is to wait. Once the attacker is in the area the goalkeeper should advance towards him in order to give him less goal to aim at; standing tall, using his hands to great advantage.

Perhaps Zubizarreta was guilty of this error more than most as he was sent off several times for both club and country. The last time this happened to him was on the opening day of the '96-'97 season. Valencia were in the lead against Racing de Santander, when Alberto broke clear of the defense 30 yards from goal. The defenders had time to recover the situation but Zubizarreta did not give them the chance, instead he rushed out of his area to challenge the attacker. Alberto decided to shoot from outside the box and Zubizarreta pushed the ball to safety with his hand. He was sent off for a deliberate hand ball and Valencia went on to lose the match.

16. This type of calamitous mistake is all too frequent in the game and the goalkeepers do not seem to realize that they are doing anything wrong. Worst still is the fact that the coaches and soccer commentators rarely notice this serious flaw in a player's game. A serious repercussion is that young-sters are now copying this type of erroneous intervention that goes against all the 'logic' of the sport and so it is becoming a normal part of the game. A few years ago a Racing goalkeep-er took a goal-kick and tried to pass to one of the wingers who was playing quite deep. The pass was poor and so was intercepted by a player in the other team who found himself in space some 30 yards from goal. Unbelievably, the goalkeeper took it upon himself to sprint out of the box in order to challenge the player on the ball before any of the defenders had a chance to intervene. I made reference to this move at the end of the match and asked the goalkeeper where he got the idea for such a move? To my surprise, he replied: "From Buyo! I saw him do it last night in Logroño". Of course he was perfectly right. The previous night the whole of Spain watched on television as the Madrid goalkeeper performed the eccentric move.

THE NEW TRAINING METHODS

Now let's look at how young goalkeepers and adults train. What is clear is that the goalkeeper's job description has changed over recent years and so the training programs have also evolved to best meet the requirements of the modern game. Perhaps this is why goalkeepers and coaches alike will both be surprised by thoughts and ideas on the subject.

But I am also perplexed when I see the training methods used by certain coaches. The type of work they do is neither the most practical nor the most appropriate as it has little to do with what the goalkeeper has to do in a real match.

Here is an example of some of the fundamental concepts that are omnipresent during these training sessions:

a) The training sessions are usually carried out by ex-goalkeepers as it seems that only players who have played in this position are qualified to coach it. I thought the most important thing was knowledge, understanding of the game and being able to communicate your ideas. Unfortunately, these ex-goalkeepers train their disciples using the same criteria and methods they used in their playing days. This means that the modern goalkeepers continue to train in isolation, doing traditional exercises where they learn little about how to dominate the 18-yard box and techniques and tricks employed by attackers remain a

The Evolution of the Goalkeeper

Until recent years it was inconceivable that a goalkeeper would have to play beyond his 18-yard box. Today, goalkeepers do this with such regularity that often unnecessary goals result because of it.

When I arrived at Barcelona I encouraged the youth team defenders to push up on various occasions to put pressure of the opposition's attack. The key to this tactic was the 'offside' trap and the ability of the goalkeeper to play beyond his 18-yard box effectively.

The fans were always both surprised and perturbed every time the goalkeeper advanced so far up the pitch and they could not understand: "How can he leave his goal totally unguarded." One day as I was making my way to the dugout I saw the goalkeeper Corral standing with his back to me and talking to two guys. As I got closer it was impossible not to hear what they were talking about. One of the men asked him: "But why do you play so far from your goal even beyond the 18-yard box at times?" "Are you mad?" And with a look of resignation Corral replied: "I do what I'm told. If anyone is mad it's the person who gives me the orders."

As you can see the role of the goalkeeper has undergone a tremendous evolution.

Everyone who witnessed this type of move (started 25 years ago by Corral) thought the goalkeeper and the coach had lost their sanity. This type of intervention is common-place in today's game.

mystery to them. I think goalkeepers should spend at least 80% of each training session simulating 'real' match situations so that they can experience and practice the movements and tactics involved as these are not as straight forward as they seem.

b) The defense, for example, has a very important dual function to perform. They often make the goalkeeper's life a lot easier by playing well and stopping the opposition from getting close to goal but on other occasions they cause problems. Sometimes what seems an inoffensive shot that is going wide deflects off a defender and goes into the goal, leaving the goalkeeper wrong-footed. But very few people appreciate that there are always so many bodies in between the goalkeeper and the ball that he is often left totally unsighted. It is up to the goalkeeper to recognize that this problem exists and then look for ways to overcome it as best he can. This is just one of the many less obvious day-to-day difficulties that the goalkeeper has to deal with. The goalkeeper and the defenders should also coordinate their thoughts and movements; the defenders should never play too close to the goal, for example, for fear of impeding the goalkeeper. The goalkeeper should organize and shout instructions to the defense. If there is a lack of under standing between the goalkeeper and the defenders, not only does it cause numerous goals to be scored but also serious injuries can result.

c) The goalkeepers are expected to begin specialist exercises at the end or near the end of the training session when they are tired and rather than a treat it seems like a punishment. Many scientific studies have demonstrated that when technical skills and demands are placed on the body, the first to suffer from fatigue is the Central nervous System. In other words, it is always best for goalkeepers (or any player) to do any specific technical work early in the session just after the warm-up when the body is fresh and well-rested.

d) Ironically, sometimes when the goalkeepers concentrate on specialist exercises at the end of a session the outfield players play a 'small-sided' game with tiny goals. This of course is exactly the type of activity the goalkeeper should be involved in (with bigger goals!).

e) Generally the coach makes the goalkeeper perform a very physically demanding exercise program. If the coach is with a group of three then one plays in goal while the other two look on and watch (they could be doing a light exercise routine at the same time). Even when the goalkeeper in goal is clearly exhausted he is expected to continue facing shots until he can hardly stand up on his own two feet. Then the second goal-keeper does the same and the third has a turn after he has finished. This type of training makes no sense to me at all. Goalkeepers very rarely have to do anything in a match in a state of total exhaustion. Quite the contrary, as goalkeepers always have long periods in the game when they do nothing physically and as they knows that explosive power could be needed at any moment they usually keep active by doing warm up exercises in order to keep their muscles from getting stiff.

f) It is also true that individualized training programs that meet the needs of any one specific player are few and far between. In general, goalkeepers should all have a similar knowledge and understanding of what is required when playing in goal in order to perform the activity to a very high standard.

Unfortunately, we all know that this is not the case. In theory a goalkeeper should be brave and display strong character but this is not true of all goalkeepers in the game. Anyway, it is very diffi-cult to achieve these qualities on the training ground. Physical considerations such as agility, quick reflexes, coordination and technical skills like diving, passing, deflecting, punching, catching the ball and using feet but above all tactical skills such as posi-tioning, coming off the goal-line, reading the game, making cor-rect decisions are all good examples of the type of things that can be worked on in training. But every goalkeeper will have dif-ferent strengths and different weaknesses so it makes sense that they should not all be following the exact same training program. The training programs should be on an individual basis, especial-ly when learning the game because this is when the greatest differences in knowledge and skills exists. Crazy as it seems, the majority of coaches make goalkeepers follow an identical training program, rotating to practice the same routine one after the other.

g) Another thing I cannot understand is why goalkeepers are expected to face 'unstoppable' shots during training. Perhaps the coach (subconsciously) is showing his superiority over the goalkeeper or at the very least he is making sure that his goal-scoring prowess is clear for all to see. It is not pedagogically sound to shoot the ball so hard and wide of the goalkeeper that he has no chance of saving it. The best idea is to gradually increase the power and the distance away from the goalkeeper in accordance with a structured progression appropriate to the level. Apart from the fact that it is very demoralizing for the goalkeeper to see the ball fly into the back of the net time after time, if he has the possibility to save the ball then this automatically leads to the practice of other skills such as running with the ball, throwing the ball out and kicking it long etc. All of these skills and techniques add to the quality and enrichment of the training sessions.

h) Any defensive techniques are always very closely linked and lead to offensive ones. As soon as the goalkeeper claims the ball he distributes it to a teammate, with greater or less accuracy, or he takes the ball forward himself. It is always a good idea to bear in mind this correlation when planning a training program for goalkeepers so that they can develop the necessary movements and techniques and deal with any weaknesses in their game. Although it seems unbelievable, this inter-relationship between defense and attack is in my experience rarely taken into account by the vast majority of coaches. What usually happens is the coach shoots, the goalkeeper saves and that is the end of the sequence with the subsequent repetitions being the same. This is a shame because if the goalkeeper is faced by a few attackers and has a few teammates taking part in the exercise, he could develop and practice useful technical and tactical aspects of his game that he is likely to face during a real match.

i) All of the above points make me think of the following questions to put to coaches and goalkeepers alike:

1. Why during the majority of training sessions does the goalkeeper repeatedly dive to try to save the ball (whether as a specialist exercise or associated to other movements) when in reality this technique is rarely necessary during a match?

2. Why does the goalkeeper not practice the technical skills and movements that he is expected to do time after time during a match? These techniques are: catching the ball in various ways and at different heights, anticipation skills necessary to save low hard shots, a variety of different interventions, positioning and punching the ball clear etc.

The next point to address is how the goalkeeper learns the different skills and techniques he is expected to perform during a match. Do not forget that the sport in general has experienced a radical change in direction from individual moves to playing as a team and collective responsibility. The modern game demands that the players have to be comfortable interchanging positions, with good teamwork and understanding, where the more intelligent players able to 'read' the game are highly sought after. When I refer to teamwork and more cooperation and understanding I am not just talking about the outfield players. I include the goalkeeper as well as an integral part of this philosophy. Just like the outfield players, the goalkeeper needs to be able to turn defense into attack as quickly as possible and to participate fully in a great many team moves.

My point is that apart from being good in goal, a goalkeeper should be able to understand and play the game with an excellent technique at a level similar to (but usually slightly less than) that of the outfield players.

I am not just referring to technique and ball skills in isolation. The goalkeeper should never separate good technique from tactical awareness and the ability to play with intelligence or else he will never become a 'complete' player. The goalkeeper can only show his true worth if he has the necessary technical skills needed to overcome all the situations he is likely to face throughout a long season.

Over recent years the modern game of soccer has undergone a tremendous evolution and so it seems only logical that training methods should also change. This evolution has affected the position of goalkeeper more than any other and so the training methods should also be radically different from years ago.

WHEN IS THE BEST TIME TO START TRAINING AS A GOALKEEPER?

It is very important that young players do not start to specialize as goalkeepers or in any one position during the 'playing for enjoyment' stage when the children are between 7-10 years old. Playing in goal requires a special training program beyond that of the normal exercises and routines as specific movements and tactical considerations are involved, but only when only when the time is right. At this young age all the children experience playing in every position, including playing in goal. This has two positive benefits:

1. *The player gets an overall grounding and understanding and acquires the necessary knowledge to be able to anticipate and 'read' the game.*

2. *The coach has time to evaluate the players in each position and decides which in his judgment is the best for the future.*

Over the years I have seen many children between the age of 6-8 only interested in playing goal After 4-5 years they become disillusioned and begin playing as outfield players but because this is new for them and they have not trained for it over the years they do not do well. They are never able to catch up and play at the same standard as the rest of their talented peers. On the contrary, the gap usually grows.

Another reason why youngsters should not specialize from an early age is psychological. Playing in goal requires an even temperament and a well-balanced psyche but the youngsters do not have these qualities at this stage of their development. This is why it is very difficult for them to cope with the highs and lows of the game: if they save a shot (however simple) they are hailed as heroes but if they let one in (even if the shot is unstoppable) they are called clumsy and hopeless. This is why youngsters should not specialize in goal and should wait until they are older when on an individual basis, players will be deemed ready thanks to their maturity and quality.

Some coaches believe that even very young goalkeepers should play in a regulation size goal so that they can get used to moving from post to post and familiarize and control the space around them. I strongly disagree. There is plenty of time for these players to get used to the dimensions they have to defend but if they start too early when the task is little short of impossible many players leave the game because of the demoralization of physically not being able to cover the immense wide open spaces above them or to either side. Nevertheless, this is still a common practice and in Spain, other sports like basketball and handball are more than delighted to welcome these children into their ranks. None of Spain's great goalkeepers over the years from Zamora, Iribar, Eizaguirre, Ramallets, Carmelo to Arconada ever played in a regulation size goal at a very young age. Normally, the goalposts were school books (probably rucksacks or school bags today) 3-5 yards apart. This distance was roughly worked out by judging how far the goalkeeper could reach according to his height. Playing under these conditions never did these players any harm. Quite the contrary, as they all played at the highest level from a very young age.

The young modern goalkeepers starting out in the game who play in regulation size goals have an almost impossible task to try to stop the well-placed shots that are stroked gently to either side of them or they are bombarded by high shots that they cannot reach (sometimes the ball even bounces in front of them and bounces over their head and goes into the goal). Under these cir-cumstances, many young goalkeepers are ridiculed by their teammates (this is something they often copy from their parents) as they are unable to reach such 'simple shots'. This treatment continues until the young goalkeepers reach an age when all the taunts and jokes affect them and they subsequently leave the game and some even suffer from psychological illnesses which are very difficult to overcome (I am not trying to alarm anyone but unfortunately I know of such severe cases).

During the 11-13 stage the would-be goalkeeper continues to play both as an outfield player and in goal, alternating between each. If the coach is convinced that the player is cut out to be a goalkeeper then he starts to do some specific training to help him improve in this position while at the same time he continues to do the usual exercises with the rest of his teammates. I have commented on this before but it is so important that it is worth repeating again. Goalkeepers intervene with their feet 66% of the time and so it is imperative for them to play and train as outfield players as much as possible. The other reason why this is so important is so that they can get a real awareness and understanding of the game and of the errors the defenders are likely to make and also what adversaries are likely to do. The goalkeeper will also be fully aware of what positions a striker needs to take up in order to produce a certain shot and what, under normal circumstances, is possible or likely to occur. All this helps the goalkeeper tremendously, but I am sure if he always has his back to the goal and never experiences playing as an outfield player himself, he will never fully appreciate and understand the game.

The overall training program is performed alongside the specific goalkeeping exercises but as the learning process is so extensive and varied it is divided up into achievable parts, starting with easy and basic concepts and leading on to the more difficult and complicated routines. There are few technical elements at first as these are practiced during a sustained period at a later date when the player concentrates on more challenging and complicated skills. The familiarization period (when few technical skills are practiced) may last for up to 3 weeks, but this varies depending on the learning ability of the particular group of players.

The first thing the goalkeeper is taught is manual dexterity in all its many shapes and forms. The goalkeeper first learns that it is relatively straightforward to gather the ball with the hands but that using his feet is far more complicated. The goalkeeper practices using his hands time after time (there is no mystery to this) until he masters all the movements and coordination.

Here is some general advice on this:

a) When catching the ball in the hands make sure a part of the body is always behind them backing up. On certain occasions (slippery ball or poor positioning of the hands etc.) the ball is spilled or slips between the hands, but if legs, stomach, chest or even head are positioned behind as back up then a goal is avoided. Always follow this simple rule "Any intervention with hands should always be backed-up with a part of the body".

b) When catching the ball at chest height, one foot should always be slightly in front of the other with the weight on the former. Lean slightly forward and when the ball arrives gather it and clutch it to the chest with forearms and hands. As the ball is being gathered, move the weight onto the back foot to help soften the blow.

c) If the ball arrives neck-high then the goalkeeper jumps and follows the same procedure as above. To execute this catching technique perfectly the leading leg should always be slightly bent as it is performed.

d) If the ball arrives at such a height that it is impossible to get any part of the body behind it then the arms need to be outstretched with both hands behind the ball and the fingers extended. If the shot is very powerful then it is advisable to move the fingers back slightly at the moment of impact to soften the blow.

e) It is common to see young goalkeepers dive when a ball heads towards the body or slightly to the side of them to make the save look more spectacular. Never do this.

If for any reason the ball is dropped then it is always easier for the goalkeeper to rectify the situation if he is on his feet because he can pounce on the ball. However, if the same thing happens and the goalkeeper is already on the ground then the likelihood is that he will not get to the ball in time and a goal will result.

The outfield player has to do incessant ball-juggling skills in order to be totally comfortable on the ball so that he is able to perform the necessary technical executions during a match. In the same way, the goalkeeper has to practice manual dexterity and balls skills with his feet over and over so that he too is ready to perform at the highest level during games. Of course there are no shortcuts and the only way to improve skill levels and reach the top is by constant practice. The young player needs to dedicate hour after hour to this type of practice, especially when training on his own at home, which is something I cannot recommend highly enough.

DEVELOPING A GOALKEEPER'S "TOOLS"

All of the manual dexterity training should be carried out without gloves. Adults should wear gloves (many of the frequent finger injuries that used to plague goalkeepers have disappeared because of their use) but this is not recommended for beginners. Fingers can only be strengthened properly, a good feel for the ball and a secure catching technique can only be achieved with direct contact with the ball.

I have coincided on various occasions with Iribar when we were both guest speakers at conventions on Grass roots soccer. He is a real expert on the subject of goalkeeping and this is how he replied to my question about the use of gloves: "I am not in favor of youngsters using gloves. During this crucial learning stage the payers have to perfect the correct catching technique and it is vital that they come into direct contact with the ball. We are lucky in the Basque country because we play frontón which helps develop strong hands and fingers plus quick reflexes". I also think that the game of basketball is good for anybody hoping to play in goal as it involves continuous and rapid movements, with short runs, twists and turns and jumps. Add to this the fact that it requires a tremendous tactical awareness as the players have to take up positions anticipating the movements of the opposition and defense is turned into attack very quickly and vice versa. These are all basic requirements that this sport has in common with the game of soccer. A quick and enjoyable game of basketball can always be incorporated into a training session to energize the players after a par-ticularly tedious and tiring session.

Iribar, a genuine talent.

I do not recommend the game of handball for goalkeepers. Although it is true that this sport involves many techniques and movements useful for a goalkeeper, such as a good throwing arm, competitiveness, the ability to 'read' the game and a good sense of positioning, it all too frequently produces shoulder, elbow, knee and particular finger injuries.

Nor do I recommend that goalkeepers should play in goal in handball games. This is because the size of the goals and the surface under foot are totally different from soccer. Also, catching technique is not a fundamental ability in this sport, whereas in soccer it is imperative.

There are two sports that I thoroughly recommend for goal-keepers: table tennis and boxing. Table tennis is a very good game because it does not require a great deal of physical effort, it develops reaction speed and it involves quick adjustments of balance and the position of the feet. It is extremely useful for goalkeepers to acquire these qualities. Although boxing requires more physical effort it also involves similar skills as table tennis: quick reflexes, good positioning and footwork plus punching accuracy, power and bravery. I always encourage the players to put on a pair of boxing gloves from time to time to spar with each other (without hitting hard of course). For this reason I recommend that the players have the possibility of improving punching technique and power by having the use of a punch-bag which could be hung in the gym or any other appropriate place available.

It is important for the players to strengthen their fingers as this helps when catching the ball. A good exercise for players starting out as goalkeepers is to squeeze a small rubber ball over and over. Another good exercise is to throw a tennis ball against a wall and then catch the rebound one-handed. At first the player stands 8 yards away from the wall and gradually gets closer and closer to it. Just as with frontón, this exercise helps improve reflexes. The best time to improve and develop reaction speed is between the ages of 10 - 20. So it is a good idea to do these (or similar) exercises as often as possible during this age.

Once the goalkeeper has reached a reasonable level of competency as far as using his hands is concerned (I am not trying to imply that he has mastered all there is to know by this stage, far from it), he needs to start learning how to dive. Diving (along with competing for the ball in the air with an opponent), is the most dangerous and risky execution in the game of soccer. I have already criticized coaches for basing their training routines on repetitive diving drills and would like to clarify this point still further. Of course, the goalkeeper needs to perfect this technique because it is potentially dangerous if the player does not know how to land properly and serious injuries can result.
Nevertheless, this move is used sparingly during a match (unless the player is showing off for the crowd or the photographers) and should only be used as a last resort. This move puts the goalkeeper's physical well-being at risk and its success or failure could decide the outcome of the match so it is imperative that the goalkeeper practices the technique repeatedly in order to perfect it totally. So when I said it was not a good idea to practice diving repeatedly during training, I was referring to adults and professionals who should only dive during games. Beginners, however, should practice the technique over and over.

Before the goalkeeper learns how to dive he has to perform various exercises to help achieve the necessary neuromuscular coordination: forward and backward rolls, doing handstands, using the vaulting-horse and the box etc. This helps the player get used to the ground underfoot and move his body in the air. He also learns how to fall correctly and how to withstand minor injuries and increase his pain threshold (within acceptable limits).

Once the player overcomes the fear of hitting the ground and he knows how to move well through the air with twists and turns, he can begin to practice diving, increasing the difficulty of the exercises progressively. Nevertheless, just because he has reached this stage does not mean that he should refrain from doing the gymnastic and acrobatic exercises. Even if the player becomes a 'great' in the game and he plays for a top professional club he should still incorporate one of these routines into his training program on a weekly basis.

The basic movements of the dive are divided into four parts: impetus, take off, flying trajectory and fall. The real problem is with the last part as this is where injury is most likely to occur. The coach needs to make sure that the player fully understands the correct falling technique so that he does not harm himself as he makes contact with the ground.

The first diving exercises are very important. If the goalkeeper hurts himself on the first try, when he repeats the exercise he is inhibited by the memory of the pain. So, the first time diving exercises are carried out the following extra precautions are necessary: the player wears thick clothing, padded trousers, knee and elbow pads and the diving surface is as soft as possible (sand, grass or mat). The first thing the player is told about the landing is that the ball should make contact with the ground first, acting as an extra 'hand' to soften the fall and avoid injuries, especially to the elbows. After the ball, the thigh, hip and side of the torso land and absorb the fall.

I asked Iribar for his comments on this and he told me: "I was lucky because I played a lot of beach soccer in Guipuzcoa. This makes the beginners confident enough to dive about freely without fear of hurting or injuring themselves on landing. The movements are repeated and slowly but surely the players manage to dive and reach those balls that they couldn't reach at first."

Even though the players know how to use the dive during games, the training of this technique should be very measured, methodical and progressive. The players only move on to the next exercise when they master the previous one. Here is an example of the progression:

a) The beginner kneels down holding a ball. He dives to his left or right still holding onto the ball and making sure he concentrates on falling correctly as previously stated.

b) The same procedure is repeated from a squatting position.

c) The goalkeeper dives to his left or right from a kneeling position to save a ball that is thrown to him by the coach from a distance of 2-3 yards.

d) The same procedure is followed from a squatting position.

e) The same procedure is followed with the goalkeeper standing up with his knees slightly bent.

Sometimes, a goalkeeper new to the game, who has learned how to dive correctly thanks to the methodical training exercise program, does nothing but moan at the defenders when confronted by an attacker in a '1 v 1' shouting: "You've left me isolated!". Of course this type of attitude makes it easy for the attacker to score. Simply explain to him that if defenders were perfect there would be no need for goalkeepers. Also explain to him that in a '1 v 1' confrontation he has nothing to lose, so he should have a go. Just as with penalties, if he takes a risk and goes for it he can only gain. If a goal results, he is not criticized because that is the most likely outcome. But if he saves the day he is a hero.

Another point worth touching on is the type of clothing goalkeepers should wear. I agree that they should wear protective clothing during training (not during games because they do not have to dive very often) but gradually even this concession should be lessened as it greatly impedes speed and agility. One day at the Barcelona School I weighed one of the 11-year old goalkeepers (he was wearing gloves, knee pads, elbow pads, t-shirt, tracksuit bottoms, socks, stockings, sweatshirt, boots, two tracksuits...). His normal weight without clothes was 29 kilograms but with his kit he weighed just under 36 kilograms (6.450 kilograms more). Although it seems crazy, this 20% increase in weight is by no means an exception and of course it causes a series of problems: fatigue and lower back problems and it affects overall performance levels.

Coaches should get the novice goalkeeper used to only wearing shin pads while at the same time he should also carry a plastic bag containing a baseball cap and a towel onto the pitch with him. The weather is so changeable in Spain that it can change from beautiful sunshine to heavy rain in an instant and vice versa. Many goals have been scored over the years because the goalkeeper was left unsighted because of the mud or rain in his face. Under these circumstances the towel is very useful. In years gone by the kit man used to go to the changing rooms to get a baseball cap for the goalkeeper if he was 'blinded' by the light but often a goal was scored before he was able to put it on.

The goalkeeper is responsible for taking his own kit out with him onto the pitch and he should leave whatever he does not use in a bag near one of the posts. If for any reason he needs anything he has easy and quick access to it. The role of the goalkeeper is so important that he should try to cover every eventuality.

Something else I do not understand is why the substitute goalkeepers never warm up, even when it is cold and wet. It is far more likely these days, thanks to the new rule changes (and due to injury), that a goalkeeper will be sent off at any time during the game. If this happens, the first thing the cold and stiff substitute goalkeeper has to do is try to save a penalty or a free kick. I think it is far better for the goalkeeper to limber up and warm up with the substitute outfield players so that he is 'ready' to play.

MENTAL CONSIDERATIONS

I will finish this first section referring to novice goalkeepers by pointing out that this is the precise time that the youngsters experience the tremendous mental change and physical development brought about by puberty. It is always a good idea to get the players to do regular exercises based on psychology and relaxation. At this age the players should not be expected to undertake a physically demanding training program because their performance and energy levels are very volatile. This is a particularly dangerous period for goalkeepers because if they are inconsistent and make serious errors they could lose motivation and give up because of their lack of mental strength and maturity. The coach needs to be very aware of the situation and needs to empathize and encourage the goalkeeper, convincing him that it is just a passing phase in his development. Relaxation and motivational exercises are therefore imperative during this difficult stage of a player's development.

This stage and the next stage of the training should be supervised personally by the coach, although his staff may help out and support him. Unfortunately, many clubs still make the goalkeepers train on their own, depriving them of the vital coaching expertise and supervision that they desperately need. If the coach supervises the goalkeepers training, he has a far better idea of any strengths and weaknesses and how to accentuate the positive and eliminate the negative. Also, the goalkeepers work harder and are fully motivated trying to please the coach and become the first team choice.

Many coaches I have spoken to agree with what I have just said but they do not know the best time to train the goalkeepers. I always give the same reply: the goalkeepers should be trained just before the start of the general training session when the players and the coaches are fresh and full of motivation and energy. Once the goalkeepers have finished their session they join the rest of the team for the general training exercises. If for some reason it is not possible to carry out the specialist goalkeeper training before the general exercises then the coach and the players should agree on a specific time when this is possible, taking into account the commitments of both parties. Either way, it is very important that this training does not take place after the general exercises have finished. If this happens the goalkeepers are tired and lacking in the necessary energy and vitality they need in order to achieve their training goals.

Once the players reach the age of 14-15 (when they have good overall knowledge and technique including using hands and feet, playing in goal and as outfield players) the specific goalkeeper training is more involved and lasts longer. Make sure the players do this before the general exercises with the rest of the team, which they take part in but now in a more specific role.

In particular, they do not take part in the very physically demanding routines. During the games and 'small-sided' games they play in goal for all but 5 minutes, during which time they play as outfield players.

During the 'small-sided' games and 'rounds' carried out by the goalkeepers it is very important that they are multi-faceted, concentrating on all the necessary attributes needed to play in goal. These exercises allow the goalkeeper to develop all the technical and tactical requirements of the game plus two other very important qualities needed to play in goal: bravery and courage. These games also inspire confidence and allow the players to form their own opinions and personality based on experience and trial and error, which helps them to deal with the numerous situations they will be faced with in a real match.

It is very important that at first the goalkeepers are involved in 'small-sided' games and 'rounds' on small pitches with small goals and few players. If these exercises are performed on a big pitch with big goals and lots of players then the goalkeeper will have very few opportunities to get involved in the game and therefore learn his craft. Small pitches and goals and a game with two teams with only a few players in each allows the attackers to threaten the goal a lot more and thus the goalkeeper is kept busy. As far as the 'rounds' are concerned, a small playing area keeps the goalkeeper involved, constantly allowing him to practice a multitude of difficult movements and useful techniques. When playing in 'rounds', the goalkeeper always swaps on a regular basis with other players and takes turns playing in goal or as an outfield player. This is part of the fundamental philosophy of the 'small-sided' games and 'rounds'. The goalkeeper should be kept constantly involved and motivated so that he can perfect his technique and tactical awareness.

As soon as the goalkeeper starts playing the 'small-sided' games and 'rounds' he is continually reminded that he is the first attacker in the team and so as soon as he gets the ball he should start the attack by passing it accurately to a teammate instead of kicking the ball aimlessly as far up-field as possible and handing possession to the opposition. The idea is to identify a teammate in space and throw the ball to him or kick it to him as an alternative option in the hope that he continues the offensive move. It is important to make sure that the novice goalkeeper (this applies to all the players) understands that the best time to release the ball and start an attack is immediately after the opposition loses the ball. At this precise moment the opposition are caught momentarily out of position. So as soon as the goalkeeper gets the ball under these circumstances he should put it back in play immediately (either with a throw or a kick) before the opposition has a chance to reorganize.

This is why it is imperative for the goalkeeper to practice this move repeatedly so that he becomes a good offensive player. The goalkeeper therefore practices distributing the ball with speed and accuracy with both hands and feet during the 'small-sided' games and 'rounds'. However, if the goalkeeper has not mastered these techniques then he practices them even more when not taking part in these exercises. Hard work and dedication is the only way he can perfect and master these important technical and tactical skills.

The player continues to build on the skills he started to learn in the previous level (manual dexterity and diving) increasing the difficulty on a progressive basis. Also, other elements are introduced at this level that continue on nicely from those previously learned, plus some totally new executions and skills are introduced.

For example, the goalkeeper has to start dealing with high crosses played in behind him and in front of him so that he learns to anticipate the attacking movements of the opposition and so that he is not beaten for height. He continues to practice diving to his right or left but the degree of difficulty is increased.

The goalkeeper moves sideways and dives for balls which the coach rolls from a close distance very near to the post. Before starting this exercise the goalkeeper needs to be comfortable moving sideways as this is one of the many fundamental skills needed to play in this position. He also needs to practice relatively long sprints as he will often have to rush off his line, sometimes running beyond the 18-yard box. Running sideways is such an important skill that I am going to explain the technique involved in more detail. When a ball is heading for the goal very near to the post it is usually impossible for the goalkeeper to dive and reach the ball from his position, so he needs to take a few paces sideways in order to get into a better position. He should use a crossover movement, moving a step forward with the balancing leg with the other one in line with the direction the ball is coming from. In this way, he is able to dive as he makes the second crossways movement whereas if he shuffles across he can only dive after the third movement. It is debatable which movement is the most efficient. I always leave it to the individual goalkeeper to decide which he feels more comfortable with.

Once the goalkeeper is familiar with these movements he progresses onto the dive and deflection. This type of movement is not common in the game. However, the novice goalkeepers are obsessed with trying to hold onto the ball and rarely try to deflect wide of the goal for a corner even if this is realistically the only option open to them. The former is obviously the safest technique to use but sometimes a goalkeeper has to realize that he has no choice but to parry or deflect. Sometimes the ball is just too far from the goalkeeper for him to be able to gather it properly, or it could be very wet and therefore the slippery ball greatly diminishes the chances of a successful catch. The goalkeeper may also decide that there are too many opponents nearby in the box to risk trying to catch the ball safely and so, if in doubt, deflect it out.

Many novice goalkeepers and even professional ones have conceded goals for not listening to this advice. It is important to properly learn the dive and deflection technique as many players land on their elbow when trying this move, which is extremely dangerous. The goalkeeper should break his fall with his thigh, hip and side. The arm should be fully extended and should not touch the ground. The correct technique is to outstretch the arm nearest the ball, pushing away with the palm of the hand out for a corner or along the dead-ball line. Please note that the goalkeeper should not try this technique when standing on the goal-line as he runs the risk of scoring an own goal.

PUNCHING THE BALL CLEAR

Another technique the goalkeeper learns during this level is using his fists to punch the ball clear. Sometimes there are so many players in the area that, faced with a high ball, the goalkeeper cannot risk trying to catch the ball and so the best option is to punch it as far away from the danger area as possible. He should also use this option when he is not totally confident that he will catch the ball.

The technique is as follows: take a run up, bend slightly to get impetus for the jump, jump, outstretch the arm and meet the ball at the highest point with the fists and then land. The run up very much depends on the available space and the direction and speed of the ball. It is not essential as the goalkeeper always has a reach advantage over the attackers even with a stationary jump and outstretched arm. But if it is used then the last stride should be longer than the others. Before jumping the goalkeeper bends his body slightly to lower his center of gravity. The impetus for the jump should be off one foot but if the area is very congested then both feet are used because of the lack of space. The goalkeeper jumps higher thanks to the impetus generated by the jumping leg and by pushing down with the arms. Once in the air, the goalkeeper has both arms in front of him, bent at the elbow and he clenches both his fists. Once the player is as high as he can jump he propels his arms forward as fast as he can from the elbows and in the same movement he

When punching with both fists the area of contact should be as large as possible.

makes a clean and powerful contact with the ball. The surface area of the point of contact consists of: closed hands and both fists together forming a flat surface.

The landing should be softened by having the legs slightly parted and knees slightly bent.

When learning this technique the goalkeeper goes through the following steps:

1. First he learns how to coordinate the arm movements correctly. The goalkeeper stands with his legs slightly apart and his arms bent and his fists together. A teammate throws a ball to him from a distance of 2-3 yards and he fully extends his arms and punches it back to him. If for any reason this movement is not executed properly then the ball is removed from the exercise temporarily so that the player can practice the technique over and over again before introducing the ball back into the exercise.

2. Once the first movement is perfected the player moves onto the jump. This is practiced without the ball at first. The goalkeeper takes two paces, gets the impetus for the jump and stretches his arms as high as he can in front of his body.

3. The next step in the procedure is to use the 'suspended' ball. The goalkeeper positions himself approximately 2-3 yards from the 'suspended' ball. The height of the ball should be in accordance to the jumping ability of the player. After a short run up he jumps and punches the ball upwards with fluid and free-flowing arm movements.

When carrying out this activity the players often produce the same recurring mistakes which need to be eradicated quickly or else they convert into bad habits which are hard to address effectively at a later date:

a) A frequent error with the jump is that the players poorly time the impact with the ball with the outstretched arms. The arms are outstretched and then the punch is executed as a separate movement.

b) At the moment of impact the power is generated thanks to the spring-like action from the elbows. Some goalkeepers have their arms fully extended as they make contact with the ball. Others only use the impetus generated by the elbows after they have punched the ball away. In both these cases the ball never travels very far.

c) A poorly directed ball is almost always due to an erroneous punching technique. Maybe the goalkeeper does not form a flat and solid surface when putting his fists together. If a player is unable to clench his fists as he jumps then the coach should momentarily tie his hands together at the wrists using a blind-fold or a piece of elastic and make him practice the technique.

I think that the most important thing a goalkeeper has to do correctly (any player in fact) is positioning. A goalkeeper who is always in the right place at the right time will concede very few goals. This is why it is important to practice good positioning sense repeatedly during training. This is the right stage for the goalkeepers to start to learn this and however good they get at it they need to continue to practice it until they retire from the game. Whether or not the player is at the peak of his powers and is a full international or still playing the game at the age of 35 the most important aspect of his game remains the same: position-ing.

This is very difficult for the goalkeeper to achieve because it depends on where the ball is coming from and he constantly has to alter his position to compensate for this.

What I mean by this is that the player should stand in line with the ball, making sure he is an equal distance from both posts (if the ball is opposite the goal). If the ball is out wide then the goal-keeper still stands in the middle of the imaginary triangle formed by the ball and the two posts (but he is obviously now closer to one post than the other). Only very exceptional goalkeepers can afford the luxury of not following this guiding principal.

This angle can always be kept the same when taking side-ways steps or jumps without turning the feet as these should

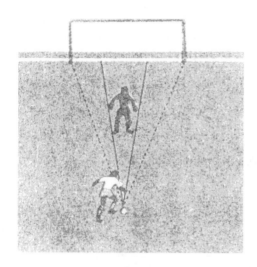

The goalkeeper is positioned correctly between the posts. The shooting angle gets smaller and smaller as the goalkeeper gets nearer to the attacker.

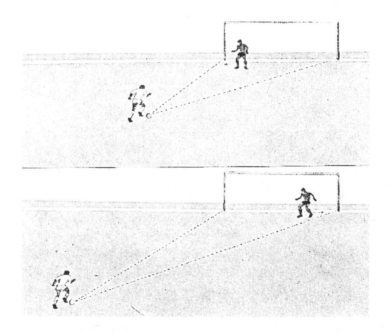

By contrast, the goalkeeper is too far back and out of position in these examples.

always be pointing in the direction of the ball. When moving sideways it is important that the right leg moves first when moving to the right and the left first when moving to the left. The steps should always be short, even though this means the goalkeeper has to take more of them because in this way the body weight is always evenly distributed and the goalkeeper is always well balanced. If for any reason the goalkeeper takes longer steps (everything is always possible in this game) then he will have to reposition himself, but this takes longer because one of his feet is off the ground for a longer period of time. Normally what happens under these circumstances is that the goalkeeper does not have as much time to adjust his position as he would like.

Also taking longer steps can take the goalkeeper out of position because there was no need to move so far across. If the ball moves 1 yard across the pitch the goalkeeper only has to adjust his position 15 inches.

It has to be drilled into the young goalkeepers that during training they need to concentrate totally on the game and change their position and react in order to try to compensate for the ever changing circumstances as best they can. This is how the goalkeeper is able to perfect his positioning, technique and his overall understanding and appreciation of the game. The goalkeeper needs to be taught from the word go that he also has to help control and organize his defenders. In this early stages a mark is located in between the two posts to help the goalkeeper position himself correctly.

It is very important for the goalkeeper to have good orientation and spatial awareness skills. If he has these his positioning will be correct and this will undoubtedly help his performance. The training program for the goalkeeper involves games and 'small-sided' games that allow him to develop and perfect this fundamental skill. From wide crosses the goalkeeper should position himself somewhere on the goal-line and ¼ distance from the far post and ¾ distance from the near post. If the ball heads for the near post then the goalkeeper has more ground to cover but at least he can do it quickly.

If the ball heads towards the far post then he is close enough to it to run backwards and claim it. If the ball goes beyond the far post then the goalkeeper turns and gets ready to save any shot he might receive at what is now his near post. I have seen lots of goals scored from wide crosses and all because the goalkeeper was positioned at the near post.

Now is the right time in the goalkeeper's development to start to teach him how to position the wall and where to position himself against free-kicks. The goalkeeper stands at the post closest to the ball and he draws an imaginary line from this position to the ball. This is where he positions his 'marker' defender and then the others stand next to him, moving progressively towards the center of the pitch. Once this side of the goal is correctly protected by the wall the goalkeeper moves across to cover the other side. Let me make it clear that he does not position himself in the middle of the goal but towards the other half of the goal that is not protected by the wall. The goalkeeper has to insist that all his teammates drop back and help out. They are all indispensable and potentially goal-saving players in these situations.

When his team is attacking and the ball is in and around the opposition's penalty box, the goalkeeper should move forward off his line. He should move right up to the edge of the 18-yard box. This is so that he can run out of his area to clear any long ball that results from a quick counter-attack before the opposing striker has a chance to get to it. If the opposition mount a more measured attack then the goalkeeper moves back and relays messages and instructions to his defenders while at the same time always changing his own position depending on the location of the ball.

At this level, any training the goalkeeper does at home is particularly beneficial. The player should take advantage of all the time he spends away from the training ground to methodically perform a wide range of exercises . These activities could involve basic stretching and balancing exercises, playing in a make-shift goal as friends shoot at him or practicing ball skills (relevant to both the goalkeeper and the outfield player). One of these skills should be heading practice but without opposition at this stage.

As I mentioned earlier the goalkeeper needs to be able to master this technique during the game. Obviously he also needs to spend time trying to correct and perfect any weaknesses in his game that are apparent on the training ground.

FOCUSING ON PHYSICAL DEVELOPMENT

Once the goalkeeper reaches the age of 14-15 his physical development is very different. Early developers may seem fully developed by this age whereas the long-limbed and gangly may only look 11 years old. It is always useful to be conscious of this fact in the context of soccer and especially when referring to goalkeepers. The coach is responsible for not only having an excellent knowledge and understanding of soccer but also of physiology. I have seen many early developers produce some fantastic performances at the age of 14, often helping the team win lots of matches. Unfortunately, none of these players ever make it as professionals because although they were big compared to most other 14 year olds, they usually stop growing at a young age and are quickly caught up and passed by other players.

If psychological exercises are very useful for the outfield players, imagine the benefits for the goalkeeper, who has a far more complicated mission to complete. It is no surprise to me that goalkeepers often seem a little eccentric and mentally unstable. In the previous level the goalkeepers started to carry out relaxation and motivational exercises whereas now they should dedicate a lot more time to these plus add more concentration-related activities. This is imperative when playing in this position.

In my experience, goalkeepers are able to withstand more intensive training programs than outfield players without affecting their performance and physical condition. I think that goalkeepers should train more than the other players, to be exact 3 or 4 hours more a week, as long as the training is carried out in a rational and methodical way. It is not true that goalkeepers lose form as a result of too much training. It is important to highlight that their physical condition the day after a match is very different from that of the outfield players. While the goalkeeper is able to play another match in top shape, the outfield players' physical condition is not the best, they are tired and are recovering from stiff muscles, which means not only would they perform badly but also they would run the risk of picking up an injury. So, it makes sense that the goalkeeper is able to train longer and more intensively.

At this level of perfection, the goalkeeper's training should increase gradually, until, as an adult, he reaches the level I have just recommended. For the moment he continues his weekly program, coupled with what he did at the previous level. Plus, he will also start to carry out individual training sessions "at home" which I recommend separately to the outfield players. The basis of these sessions for the goalkeeper (which will also last 20 minutes), will continue to be gymnastic exercises, but the time spent running disappears to be replaced by some elemental acrobatic exercises. He will also carry out specific training, completely separate from his teammates. He does this on the day the rest of the players have their day off.

At this level the technical moves that the goalkeepers have learned in previous years will only be practiced in 'rounds' and 'small-sided' games. But, if he makes some repeated mistakes during his participation in such games, the coach will make a note of them and then will suggest he carries out and perfects these techniques during the specific training (using the 'suspended ball' or the 'wall'), until he is satisfied that the goalkeeper has corrected them. For example, a common mistake at this age is for the goalkeeper to land on his elbows or abdomen when diving. At this level one of the moves which should be perfected is the clearing the ball with the fists. This is not as easy as it sounds. As the contact surface with the ball is small, it is not easy to always get it right. Also, if the goalkeeper punches the ball and it stays in play, it could produce an even more dangerous situation. In spite of this, it is a useful and valuable technique. I would go as far as to say that it is indispensable.

The goalkeeper should try to get the ball, but not at any price. If he sees that it is not safe to catch the ball, he should clear the danger by punching the ball away with his fists.

Up to now I have talked about the clearance with both fists because, with the determining factors I have just explained, it is the most appropriate as far as safety and effectiveness are concerned. But if the goalkeeper does not have space to jump or sees that he can not reach the ball with both fists, then he should make the clearance with one fist only. The contact surface he uses for this is the tips of the fingers. This technique enables the goalkeeper to stretch higher, above the heads of the rest of the players (both the defenders and the attackers), who jump for the ball, but it is very risky due to the small contact surface, which is why I recommend it only be used when it is impossible to use the two-fisted clearance.

At this level, to perfect the moves I have been commenting on, the following aspects should be worked on:

1. The 'suspended ball' should be swinging and positioned in such a way that the goalkeeper can only hit it by jumping, when the rope is vertical. So the goalkeeper has to choose the right moment to jump and strike the ball exactly.

2. The direction of the ball cleared by the fist or fists should also be controlled. The ball should generally be aimed to the opposite side to that from which it came. If it is knocked towards the center or towards the central zone, the goalkeeper could find that the ball is returned and ends up in the net before he is back in position.

3. It is also advisable for the clearance to be high. While the ball is going up and coming back down the goalkeeper and his teammates can reposition and organize themselves. But if the clearance is low or towards the ground, an opponent could get the ball and shoot immediately.

4. Once he has mastered this, the goalkeeper should practice the clearances against opponents, who jump and compete with him, trying to beat him to the ball.

5. I know from experience that some goalkeepers take a run up from some distance before punching the ball clear. The jump is

more long than high and this is why the opponent gets to the ball first and many goals result. The goalkeeper has to make sure the force of the jump is upwards. If he does not jump correctly the coach should make him practice the jumps repeatedly at the 'suspended ball', after showing him the take off and landing zone on the floor.

I have explained that the goalkeeper should also know how to control the ball with his head, for which he will have carried out the relevant training. At this level he practices headers with a teammate, jumping and diving to get the ball first. In these particular 'small-sided' games (in which only the head is used), he plays as an outfield player but when it is his turn to go in goal, whenever possible, he only uses his head to save the ball from going into the net. The goalkeeper also carries out exercises or games involving teammates and opposition where only the head is used, where the players on his own side sometimes help and, unfortunately, sometimes hinder. These prepared moves and 'set plays' are carried out inside and outside the area. The advantages and disadvantages of using one or two fists (which I have just explained) are also valid for the head clearance. If the goalkeeper jumps or dives against opponents, he is able to reach further with his fists but he has a greater contact area using his head (although he has more chance of getting injured). Some goalkeepers head exceptionally well and others do not dare use their head. I recommend that when the goalkeeper is forced to head outside the area with an opponent near that he should try to send the ball out of play. In this way he avoids the possibility of a quick goal being scored and he and his teammates have time to reposition themselves.

Even though jumping (catching, clearing with fists or head) is difficult to master, it allows the goalkeeper to not only gain control of the ball but also of the space around him. This skill involves some other very important qualities: coordination, balance and leg strength, especially in the thighs. The aforementioned qualities have to work correctly and in perfect unison in order to achieve success in getting the ball. If the goalkeeper wants to noticeably improve this aspect of his game, he needs to repeat the jumping and diving movements over and over again, during the training sessions, month after month, year after year.

THE SMALL BUT VERY SIGNIFICANT DETAILS

Of course, the minor details are equally important and valuable in order to be a great goalkeeper. For example, if an opponent has the ball close to the corner the goalkeeper should be ready to come out and intercept the cross. But success will depend (apart from the difficult qualities previously referred to) on the position of the goalkeeper's feet. If they are pointing towards the person who has possession of the ball, his quick exit off his line could be too late and in vain. On the other hand, if his feet point towards the central circle his movements to intercept the pass will be very successful as his body is already facing the direction of the run.

There is another detail which I consider to be of greater value than that normally given to it: When the goalkeeper comes out (or indeed in all moves involving them), he should shout for the ball by saying something like 'Goalkeeper's ball' 'I'm coming', 'Mine', 'Me!' or something similar as a warning. In the first place the shout distracts the forward, and if he is already a bit nervous he panics even more, as now all his attention is on the ball, perhaps on the defenders and on what he is going to do. In fact, his teammates sometimes cause more of a problem than the opposition. When the goalkeeper comes off his line all his attention is focused on the ball and his opponents, but he mistakenly forgets to worry about his own defenders. As far as the defenders are concerned, they do not see the goalkeeper as they are concentrating on the attackers and are only interested in getting to the ball as quickly as possible. In these cir-

"Goalkeeper's ball!"

cumstances, anything can happen, from the goalkeeper getting the ball, to a defender clearing the ball to safety. But unfortunately, the following also occur with regularity:

1. When the goalkeeper is about to pick up the ball, a defender kicks it into his own goal or just makes enough contact on the ball to leave it at the feet of one of the players in the opposition.

2. The defender gets in the way of the goalkeeper involuntarily, which helps an opponent get to the ball first.

3. The goalkeeper and defender crash into each other and fall, which ends up as another gift for the opposition.

4. The clashes between goalkeeper and defender cause such serious injuries that players (and I know of various cases) have had to give up the game.

90% of the problems I have just outlined can be avoided by the goalkeeper simply warning when he's going for the ball. I recommend that coaches teach this simple but tremendously important aspect of the game from the previous stage. This is done by getting the goalkeepers to shout for the ball when they are going to claim it. They should do this in the games, small-sided' games and 'rounds' or any exercise that they carry out during training. (to make this even clearer: I am referring to coming for the ball and the exercises they carry out when in goal. Ideally the goalkeeper should shout automatically, in the same way as he automatically shouts instructions to his players concerning any other technical or tactical move).

However, the mere fact that the goalkeeper shouts for the ball does not automatically mean that that the defender has to leave it. There are occasions when the goalkeeper realizes that he cannot get to the ball, or even if he gets to it that he could be beaten by an opponent. In both cases a good goalkeeper will warn his teammates so that they still have time to deal with the ball quickly and effectively.

Diving is a very important strategy for a goalkeeper. If he decides to launch himself it is because there is a real danger of a goal being scored. If his judgment and timing are good he avoids a goal being scored, but if he fails a goal is almost inevitable. Therefore, the goalkeeper must be in control of the situation so that he knows when to dive and when to 'hold back'. The teaching of this technique will continue at this level, though the coach needs to give theoretical classes to the goalkeepers before going on to the practical stage. As far as the theory is concerned, I get the goalkeeper to use ropes as a guide to get into the correct position. For example, if the ball is on the penalty point, the ropes stretch from that point to the two posts, with the goalkeeper placing himself in the middle of the triangle and as close to the ball as possible.

If the attack comes from the sides, the ropes change position accordingly, with the goalkeeper occupying a central position and moving towards the ball. Once he learns this, the goalkeeper is taught the unwritten rule that he should never be beaten at the near post. I also recommend during these moves in the games, small-sided' games or 'set moves', that the goalkeeper stretch out his arms and touch the near post for the following reasons:

1. To check that he is correctly positioned. If he touches the post he reassures himself that he is neither too close nor excessively far from it.

2. After touching the near post, he then moves forwards a few inches, so that if he has to dive towards the said post to intercept a shot at goal, he knows that he is far enough off his line not to collide with the post.

The '1 v 1' confrontations involving the goalkeeper and an opponent are such an important topic that I think it wise to make a series of recommendations:

1. The goalkeeper must take advantage and move forward quickly when the attacker is about to get the ball. But he must be well prepared so that when the attacker shoots, he is completely still. If for example he is moving forwards at the time of the shot it will be much more difficult to clear or catch the ball.

2. This was in fact one of Puskas´ secrets. If he found himself in a situation where he could shoot at goal and he saw the goalkeeper run towards him, he shot immediately with the instep, keeping it low and with relatively little power it always went agonizingly close to the goalkeeper. Although under these circumstances the goalkeeper was expected to save the ball, he was usually unable to react quickly enough, with the result that by the time he dived the ball had gone agonizingly close to him but past him.

3. When the goalkeeper moves forward correctly and stops 4 - 5 yards in front of the shooter, he narrows the angle and offers a much smaller target to shoot at. In spite of this, the goalkeeper, possibly I think in ignorance, throws himself to one side; the side where he thinks, due to the position of the attacker or because of his style of play, that the ball will be aimed. If he gets the ball, it was a waste of effort , as the ball was going out anyway. But, other times, the ball is only parried and with the goalkeeper on the ground, the second attempt is a goal. Also, many goals squeeze under the goalkeeper's body or outstretched arms because he leaves a gap as he dives. The goalkeeper should stay calm and keep his nerve. He should bend his knees a little to lower his center of gravity and outstretch his arms as much as possible. Psychologically this makes the attacker panic and he shoots the ball wide.

4. I want to emphasize that the goalkeeper should not launch himself when he comes out of the goal. If an unmarked opponent is about to come into the area with the ball, the goalkeeper should immediately run towards him to narrow the angle and make the goal seem smaller. If the attacker gets ready to shoot, the goalkeeper should stop sharply. This is correct, as I said before. But sometimes, the attacker loses control of the ball a little. Under these circumstances the goalkeeper should take advantage of this fraction of a second to dive and claim the ball. He should dive forwards and while his hands try to get the ball, he should raise his shoulders slightly to protect his head.

5. The goalkeeper should be shown that when he comes forwards (say 8 yards from the goal line) and the attacker is getting ready to shoot from 4 or 5 yards away, if he is well positioned and the attacker has the ball on the ground, if he wants to score a goal he will have to shoot the ball very close to the goalkeeper keeping the ball very low. If, for example, the shot is shoulder height when it passes the goalkeeper, then a goal will not result as the ball will invariably continue to rise and will eventually go over the crossbar.

6. In the '1 v 1' it is very important for the goalkeeper to be aware of the secrets which all the great goal scorers know, from experience: "The closer I get to the goalkeeper the less chance I have of scoring a goal". (In other words, get as close as you can to the striker. The move produced by Puskas is the exception to the rule).

"If the goalkeeper comes off his line and stands tall in front of me, I feint and dummy the shot to provoke him to dive to this side. Once he is committed, I kick the ball to the other side of him into the empty net. If he is not fooled, I shoot on the second backlift". (In this case, the goalkeeper should keep his nerve and not dive prematurely. He should wait and see.).

7. In the summer of´96 I was lucky enough see Iribar again at a Soccer Congress in Santander. It was a privilege to see him give practical training sessions on how to deal with the '1 v 1': always moving forwards, legs well bent, taking short steps, hardly lifting his feet off the ground and waiting without committing himself to the dive.

Some expert goalkeepers, when they see it is touch and go to beat their opponent, dive to the side, stretching their legs and arms as far as possible. If the dive is well executed and well timed, the body brushes the ground, and the ball is deflected or parried by some part of their body.

I want to make it clear that it is a move that should be used as a last resort. When the ball rebounds, there is the risk that another attacker will anticipate the action and score. In this move timing is vital. I have seen astute forwards scoring brilliant goals by lifting the ball over the body of the goalkeeper who is on the ground. However, this has less to do with the skill of the attacker, and more to do with the goalkeeper's failure to coordinate the movement properly: either he launched himself too soon or from too far away.

Now I will make reference to curling shots and passes. Of course, I have talked about and demonstrated this type of shot to the goalkeeper in the previous levels. From this level on the goal-keeper must practice it continuously and with hands as much as with feet.

The first thing which the goalkeeper must do is know about and control the complexity of this move and its application in the game, based on the 'logic' of soccer. In reality it is very difficult for the goalkeeper to know when his opponent is likely to put swerve on the ball (he can use the inside or the outside of the foot), and it is difficult to calculate the height, speed, distance and angle of the ball. It is also very difficult to know the right moment to react and which technique to use to save the ball.

The goalkeeper will dedicate a lot of time to this move, con-stantly repeating the actions against a wall. He shoots against it trying to put the correct swerve on the ball and then using his hands to try to catch it (this is very difficult to master). He must also know how to use his feet when faced by a swerving ball, which is perhaps even more complicated. I have seen some well known goalkeepers come out of their area and totally misjudge the flight of a swerving shot. Some even make positional errors by not anticipating the logical direction of the ball once it bounces.

The Goalkeeper is faced with a very difficult task when saving curling crosses or swerving shots because the rotating ball is very difficult to control. For this reason I recommend that if the goalkeeper is in any doubt when trying to save a swerving cross, he should punch it clear using two fists instead of trying to catch the ball. As far as curling shots are concerned, he should try to deflect or parry the ball with his palm, fist or forearm, trying to make it go parallel to the goal line or directly out for a corner (it is always better to concede a corner than a goal).

I think it is very important for the goalkeeper to release the ball as quickly as possible. Many goals start this way in the modern game. There is a determined effort to concentrate on this technique and tactic during this level and by the end of it the goalkeeper should have perfected this type of distribution. Nevertheless, some goalkeepers never fully master it no matter how much they practice the move.

Any goalkeeper who really sees himself as the first line of attack manages to understand and produce this move and so when he gets possession of the ball he is aware of the position of his teammates and of his opponents and immediately distributes the ball with his foot or his hand. In the past, some goalkeepers never released the ball quickly because they were obsessed with bouncing it. They picked up the ball, looked at the ground, bounced the ball, looked again, bounced again and when they eventually decided to release the ball the opposition were all correctly positioned and ready to claim it. This is not possible now because of a recent rules change. The current rule for goalkeepers is as follows:

When the goalkeeper has the ball in his hands, he can hold onto it and take as many steps as he likes for a maximum of 6 seconds. He is not allowed to drop it to the ground and pick it up again or else concedes an indirect free kick. The only time the goalkeeper can bounce the ball is immediately before he kicks it.

However, even though I have just suggested that the goalkeeper should release the ball immediately, I want to make it clear that this should not be taken to the letter. Very occasionally the goalkeeper should hold the ball for the full 6 seconds, especially if the team is going through a critical moment (perhaps a teammate has taken a blow or because there are only a few minutes left and the team is winning).

How should the goalkeeper distribute the ball? Some think that he should always throw the ball out whereas other prefer that he kicks it. The best solution is to use an intelligent mixture of the two, depending on the situation in the game and the position of the players. This variety is far more effective and makes the game more entertaining.

I suggest an intelligent mixture of the two, because if the dominating team loses the ball and the opposition launches a counter-attack from a distance using only a few players, if the ball gets to the goalkeeper it is not particularly effective to immediately send it back up the pitch because the majority of the opposition are well-organized and in position. Neither is the goalkeeper acting wisely if he insists on making a short pass to a teammate when his team is being attacked and he finds himself under siege with the opposing team attacking in numbers.

It is obvious that in the first case the ball should be thrown out short, aiding the attack. In the latter, quite the opposite is true. Given the fact that the opponents are attacking, leaving lots of free space behind them, the pass should be long and high, allowing the few attackers and defenders to compete for the ball. If the team has a 'set play' prepared for these circumstances, it may very well end in a goal.

The goalkeeper should continue to get a 'feel' for the ball and be comfortable on it by continuing to perform ball skills using hands, feet and head in a mixed and varied fashion. I know from experience that critics suggest that this type of training bears no relationship to what takes place in a match but I maintain that it increases skills, improves feet movement and develops great coordination and balance. It also gives the player tremendous belief and self-confidence on the ball. In fact the goalkeeper should never stop doing ball-juggling skills or acrobatics in his training routines. He should practice over and over again. Practice makes perfect.

PSYCHOLOGICAL PREPARATION

Psychologically this is a very delicate and complicated age (the same is true for the outfield players). The ideal age for developing the neuro-motor skills is over. In order to improve now

64

Chilavert assures us: "I am the best goalkeeper in the world." What is certainly true is that he has more self-confidence that anyone else.

the goalkeeper has to rely on willpower, tenacity and the desire to be the best. Willpower and determination is incredibly important for goalkeepers as without it many mistakes are produced that invariably cost goals. This drive and motivation is closely linked to self-confidence.

The goalkeeper needs to be very psychologically and mentally 'strong' if he wants to triumph in the game of soccer. If this is not the case, a serious mistake will shatter his nerve, diminish his confidence and after the first mistake, more mistakes will certainly follow. If he is confident and has plenty of willpower, he is able to overcome these inhibiting factors and can use his skills to the full, whether in training or in a real match.

Motivation is closely linked to concentration. If the goalkeeper is high spirited with a great appetite for the game his concentration level increases visibly. At this level the goalkeeper carries out imagination and concentration exercises to obtain the perfect combination of mental toughness and physical fitness. It is important to highlight that if he has a high capacity for concentration, he achieves quicker reaction time; remember, these mental exercises also help the goalkeeper perfect technical and tactical skills.

To sum up, from this level onwards, the goalkeeper must spend time training for the psychological side of the game, although he must never let this work affect the specific training which, of course, he continues to carry out. On the contrary, this psychological work offers a broad range of benefits on a personal and sporting level.

By the age of 19, the outfield player (who, after so many years is used to the training method), will have mastered the technical and tactical considerations during training and will have reached a certain maturity. He will have an excellent level tactically as well as a good mental state and excellent physical fitness. However, as a general rule, at this age, the same cannot be said of the goalkeeper. For this reason, I think it is advisable for the goalkeeper to continue with the previous level's training and that he should only go on to the next stage when he has learned and controlled all the relevant ideas and recommendations.

HOW MANY TRAINING SESSIONS PER WEEK?

How many days a week should a professional (or near professional) goalkeeper train per week? How many sessions should he carry out? In 'The method' the number of sessions carried out by the goalkeeper depends on age, level of aptitude and physical and mental condition. Based on that, at the highest level the goalkeeper can perform 2 or 3 sessions a day, but 48 hours before a match the best advice is to refrain from strenuous physical training. If the goalkeeper has a tough training session the day before a match, when he plays in the match he will not be at his best.

Using a 7-day cycle, 'the method' recommends (without being too rigid), that the goalkeeper does the daily morning gymnastics which he started during the previous levels. Then, the workload is spread out in such a way that the more physically demanding exercises requiring greater physical effort are carried out during the early part of the week. However, it is possible to carry out all the goalkeeper's 'specific' training on a daily basis. On Mondays he should train harder and longer (even if he has played a match on Sunday).

Tuesdays are rest days. Wednesdays are serious training days, being divided into morning and afternoon sessions. On Thursdays he has a triple session, but of a lesser intensity, approximately 75% of the previous day. On Fridays the intensity of the training continues to drop as he does 50% less than he did on the previous day. Saturday should be the day of light training, avoiding any potentially dangerous moves, to avoid picking up any injuries (coming out at a player's feet, challenging for high crosses with opponents, diving, etc.). The majority of professional games are played on Sunday in Spain, but as on every other day the goalkeeper should continue to do his gymnastic exercises.

These training sessions are done both on a collective and individual basis. The individual sessions are on Mondays, Wednesdays and Fridays the training is personally supervised by the coach. It is very important for the coach to know and improve the goalkeeper's individual strengths both in the technical-tactical and in the mental-physical aspects. As far as psychological considerations are concerned, the coach has the opportunity to get close to the player and influence and develop some of his techniques by knowing how he responds based on his temperament. As I have also repeated (but it is worth saying again), the individual training should always be done before the general team session and if it is carried out on the days that all the soccer players train, then the coach should start with the goalkeepers first, while they are still fresh and more likely to train with correct technique.

As far as the length of the sessions is concerned, youngsters should not train hard for a long time. The workload should be reduced, establishing frequent breaks between the exercises. What I mean by this is that the length of the training sessions for younger players is identical to that of adult goalkeepers, but with less intensity and the rest periods are much longer and more frequent. The length of the sessions also depends on the time in the season, the day of the week and the individual characteristics of the players. Climate is also an important consideration. If it is a hot and stuffy day the players spend less time training and a lesser intensity is necessary. When it is raining hard, the training is cut short, but more intensive. The length also depends on the number of sessions during the day. If the goalkeeper trains almost every day it is obvious that there is less practical work done, which is always advantageous. In this way it is much easier for the body to regenerate and recuperate. If the training is performed 2-3 days a week, the sessions will be much longer and more intensive.

From experience I know that playing in goal takes a lot out of the players. The continued immobility and the intense concentration are very draining. For this reason I think it is counterproductive for adult goalkeepers (who have good concentration levels)to play in goal for 2 hours. I think that one hour is sufficient, after which he should train with the rest of the outfield players. Obviously, this varies depending on the individual characteristics of each goalkeeper. Some train for 45 minutes and are very tired, while others need much more time to stay in form. This all depends on the goalkeeper's talent, his physical and mental attributes and on the type of physical effort he usually carries out and on other factors. For these reasons, the goalkeeper should never follow a set pattern.

As with normal training sessions, the goalkeeper's sessions are made up of 3 parts: The warm-up, exercises and the cooldown. Warming up should be both general and specific, preparing the player by using a series of exercises of a specific technical type, simulating the typical actions and moves performed during matches. The idea is to carry out a series of movements and actions with the ball, catches, clearances with the hand, jumps, etc.

The pre-match warm up lasts about 30 minutes and should end 5-7 minutes before the start of the match. The training will have a physical aspect, a technical aspect and finally a technical-tactical aspect. Within each of these areas, the physical effort will be very different from that done by the outfield players, which is why he should do the first two parts (physical and technical) separate from his teammates. This warm up should not leave the goalkeeper out of breath. Once this has been completed, the goalkeeper needs to stay 'warm' before the match starts by keeping on the move, which allows him to start in the best possible form.

As far as the core part of the session is concerned, firstly it is necessary to establish the specific nature of it. It can be of a technical nature, a tactical nature or a mixture of the two. In this last case, the training should be started with technical-tactical exercises, following on to ones concentrating on speed or strength. Stamina is not a specific quality needed in a goalkeeper but from time to time he will perform exercises of this type. During the training session the fundamental principle in the exercise order is that priority should be given to those which can only be done effectively when the Central Nervous System is fresh. This is the main phase and also the longest, taking up 65-75% of the session, and also it contains the greatest workload.

After a hard training session it is not a good idea to stop immediately. A sudden stop in activity can be harmful for the body, which recovers normal functions much more easily with a gradual reduction in exercise. This phase is made up essentially of relaxation exercises, involving mainly stretching and breathing activities. In other words, this is a good way of expelling the toxic substances accumulated in the body during the exercise by way of an "active rest".

In the pre-season, the goalkeeper goes back to doing all the technical moves, starting with the simplest and gradually moving on to the more complicated. Once he moves on to the season's training, I recommend that the goalkeeper practices the full range of techniques from the simplest to the most complex in a light and undemanding way. This should not last more than 15 minutes. Then the coach should highlight 3 or 4 technical elements for each session, making the goalkeeper practice them in a varied but methodical fashion. In this way he will have the time and the opportunity to become very familiar with each of the specific movements so that in the end he does them automatically and is able to correct any mistakes.

As I have repeated constantly, these exercises will only have a positive effect if the goalkeeper is mentally and physically fresh. In order to achieve this the first phase of the training should be carried out after a special warm up. It is also vitally essential that the moves are not done without stopping, one immediately after the other. The goalkeeper must have time to rest adequately and to regain his concentration. If he plays when he is physically or mentally exhausted the following may happen:

- Uncoordinated movements which lead to poorly executed techniques.

- Lack of coordination due to tiredness also increases the risk of sustaining various injuries.

-Equally, non-stop and intensive training (the goalkeeper plays at this level during a match), produces a goalkeeper with tremendous stamina but he will not perform as well as he should.

In the height of the season the goalkeeper rarely carries out training sessions exclusively for physical fitness (except the morning gymnastics and the acrobatics).During this period the incessant 'running' that coaches seem to like is unnecessary for the outfield players so it is even less relevant for the goalkeeper. Instead, the goalkeeper needs to concentrate on the type of running he needs to do during a match. Long slow runs should be replaced by short fast sprints, with changes in direction involving a series of repeated jumps. In other words, if the goalkeeper is likely to do it in a game then he should practice doing it properly in training.

HOW DO WE SOLVE TACTICAL PROBLEMS?

Some coaches and goalkeepers think that tactical problems will correct themselves in the course of the season by playing matches. I think this is a misconception. Yes, some minor things may improve when using a 'trial and error' method during the season but the only way to correct mistakes is by practicing on the training ground. During training the goalkeeper can practice the necessary techniques or moves over and over as many times as is necessary.

Some coaches also organize training sessions where one of the teams is inferior to the other and make the goalkeeper play on the weaker side so that he is more involved in the game and is put under more pressure. This does not make sense. These games serve to test and perfect the team's tactical game plan, which is why it is essential for the goalkeeper to play with his team so that he can coordinate and help organize both the defense and the attack. This also allows the coach to monitor the situation and correct the faults which always appear. What does seem sensible, however, is for the goalkeeper to occasionally play in other positions for short periods during the games and 'small-sided' games. In this way he gets valuable experience, which gives him great insight and advantages when it comes to judging distances, resolving difficult situations with his feet or head and familiarizing himself with the difficulties his defenders and attackers have to deal with.

40% of goals come as a result of a dead ball situation (free kicks (penalties, fouls with or without a wall, corners and throw-ins etc). The reason for this very probably is that in such situations the defenders (and the goalkeeper) usually make organizational errors, are out of position or lack concentration. However, it is also true that the defenders are obliged to follow certain rules at free-kicks:

- The rules do not allow them to mark the player who is about to take the kick.

- The attackers also come up in numbers putting their 'set plays' into operation.

In other words, the defending team must solve two serious problems at the same time: mark the opposition and try to control the most dangerous area of the pitch.

A good goalkeeper who positions himself correctly and has the ability to organize his teammates effectively will help to at least reduce the number of goals scored from 'dead ball' situations.

Here are some guidelines to help the goalkeeper achieve this objective:

1. Ever since I started playing the game as a youngster right up to the present day I have noticed that almost all teams (whether youth teams or professionals), if they commit a foul in their half of the pitch (could be near the area, either in the center or near the wings), all the team members, the goalkeeper, defenders; coach, etc. all have one word on their lips: "Line".

The idea is that the defenders must 'hold' the line on the edge of the 18-yard box, in the hope that they can step forward and catch a player in the other team in an 'off side' position or simply keep the opposition further from goal, giving the goalkeeper more visibility, time and freedom of movement. But I very quickly realized that this did not make a great deal of sense. If the 'free kick' is taken from a central area in front of the goal, then yes, this seems the best option, but if it is out wide then lining up in this way gives the attackers a great advantage. I often discuss this type of situation with the players during the theoretical session at the blackboard. My advice is that you place your defenders diagonally, but without them entering the penalty box. It is also fundamental that all the opposition is marked, leaving one defender free to cover for the 'short' ball and the 'near' post. This area should never be left unsupervised, as any rival could suddenly turn up there without warning.

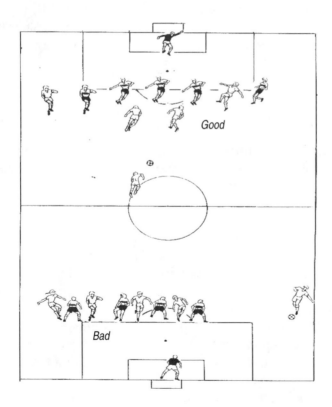

Good

Bad

The veteran goalkeeper Zoff

I was lucky enough to be in Sarria in 1982, to see the unforgettable Brazil v Italy match of 1982. There was very little time left and the Brazilians won a foul near the right touchline (see diagram bottom left), and the Italian defense stood along the edge of the 18-yard box in a flat line. The shouts (or rather bellows), from the goalkeeper Zoff, who was 40, could be clearly heard. Before the 'free-kick' was taken the game was interrupted for a substitution. I looked on and saw how Zoff took advantage of the stoppage in the game to run up to the defenders and position them properly one by one (almost dragging them where he wanted them to stand).

2. The Achilles Heel of all goalkeepers, including the best, is when they come off their line, as is demonstrated by the goals which are scored by close-range headers, as a result of the confusion caused as the goalkeeper either does not come to claim the ball or he fails to claim a cross. These moves should be practiced time after time so that the goalkeeper learns to chose the perfect moment to come off his line to claim the ball and challenge the opposition's strikers in the box.

However, to any possibility of achieving this it is fundamental that the goalkeeper has a clear space in front of him, without his teammates crowding the 6-yard box so that he has freedom of movement.

3. Following on from the previous point, it is a good idea to bear in mind that these days there are more and more players capable of propelling the ball 40 yards from a throw-in. This means that there is a serious threat on goal from these 'dead ball' situations. There is no 'off side' and the build up of players near the goal causes problems for the defenders and above all for the goalkeeper. If there is a player on the opposite team who can throw the ball this far, I recommend that the defenders not mark the opposition in the 6-yard box, but should stay outside this area. A high ball which arrives from such a distance should be left to the goalkeeper to deal with by either

catching or clearing it. What is more, if the opposition decides to throw the ball short instead and then cross it into the box, then the attackers would be clearly off-side.

4. What I have said is just as valid for corners. Nowadays many teams place their attackers on the goal line, next to the goal-keeper. As the defenders mark the attackers closely there are so many players in the 6-yard box (on occasions I have count-ed as many as 17) that it is practically impossible for the goal-keepers to intervene. Athletico Madrid won the league in 1996 by scoring decisive goals with this method, as their opponents, including the goalkeepers, were unable to find a solution to the problem. I recommend that you look at the diagram on this page and adopt the same defense.

-The player who acts as the 'wall' closing down the kicker at cor-ners needs to be tall, brave and a good jumper. He needs these qualities because he has an important mission: to make the per-son who is taking the corner nervous and lose concentration, as he knows that unless the ball is kicked high enough it will be intercepted and deflected clear.

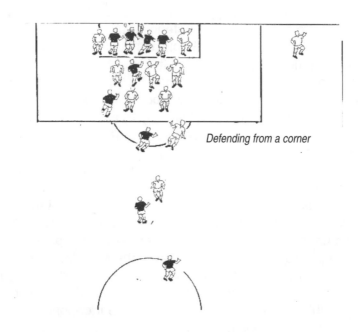

Defending from a corner

-Other tall players and good headers of the ball should be inside the 6-yard box, with one standing at the 'near' post and the other next to the 'far' post.

-Three players stand just outside the 6-yard box, filling the 'danger' zone.

-Two players stand on and around the penalty spot.

Finally two other players wait to claim any 'loose' balls from rebounds, one on the edge of the 18-yard box and the other slightly further forward.

Some teams play the corner short and gain a good advantage if the opposition does not react. Teams also take advantage by playing 'set moves' if the opposition does position a player as close as the rules allow to the player taking the corner. Under normal circumstances the player acting as the 'wall' is all that is needed to stifle any rehearsed moves but if the corner is played short to another player then the circumstances change radically as the 'feared' '2 v 1' situation arises. To avoid this, another member of the team comes across to help out but the attacker may be playing for this to happen. This is especially true if the player coming to help is the one defending the 'near post'(this is a very vulnerable area that should always be covered), as the attacker simply puts the ball there and it is met by another player running from deep. Or the ball is given to the player on the edge of the box who was waiting for any rebound or poor clearance. This type of corner is best dealt with by moving one of the players who is positioned on the edge of the 18-yard box for the rebound. But his area doesn't stay empty as it is immediately covered by the nearest player. But perhaps you are thinking: "Who is left to mark the opposition in the 6-yard box?" Of course these players should all be well marked but if the ball gets past the 'wall' then it has to be kicked high into the area. If you have reached this level and under these circumstances you are not capable of defending such a restricted area (don't forget there is also a player at each post) and your opponents cannot touch you for fear of giving away a foul, then it will be better for you to dedicate yourself to something else. Also, the position of your opponents is an advantage for the defending team:

- If the ball gets to them (but not directly), they run the risk of being caught 'off-side'.

- Also they are in a bad position to stop a swift counterattack if the possibility arises.

- There is a good chance that any clearance will be directed towards the player who is in the 'wall' (unmarked). If he receives the ball, the nearest player to him in midfield runs to play the 'one-two' while the one who was waiting on the edge of the box for the rebound runs to fill the gap in the middle and suddenly the team is on the counter filling the whole pitch.

WALLS AT 'FREE KICKS'

5. More goals are scored from 'dead ball' situations at free kicks faced by a wall than from any other 'set play'. I think, (with all due respect to the wonderful 'free kick' specialists), that the majority of these goals could be avoided if the wall was lined up properly and the goalkeeper was well-positioned. The truth is that the goalkeeper knows full well that the 'free kick' specialist is bound to shoot in one of three ways: kick the ball over the wall with the inside of his foot, or with the outside, or produce a hard shot using the toe-end of the boot, looking to place the ball towards the side of the goal supposedly covered by him. Now, the vast majority of goalkeepers do not see beyond these three options and fail to take into account or appreciate the other varieties and subtleties that could arise.

Here are some examples of what I mean:

a) Any goalkeeper playing as a top professional (or close to it), needs to be very aware that there are players with the ability to use swerve and a lot of power on the shot to curl it around the wall (to the side of the player acting as the 'marker'), and that once this happens the ball flies into the unguarded side of the goal. To avoid this the goalkeeper needs to position his 'marker' a lot further across than the youth teams (who line him up with the post), as in this way the player taking the 'free-kick' needs to defy the laws of physics in order to score with a swerving shot.

b) If the player taking the 'free-kick' positions himself very near to the ball and slightly to the side, this is a hint to the goalkeeper that the shot is likely to be 'placed' over the wall with substantial curl and little power. If on the other hand, he is a long way from the ball and takes a straight and fast run at it, then the shot will be powerful, which means the goalkeeper only has to worry about his side of the goal.

If the ball is aimed at the other side then it will almost always be stopped by the wall, go too high or be deflected clear by a player in the wall. Nevertheless, always bear in mind that there are some clever players who approach the ball in this way only to slow down when they are 2-3 yards from it in order to produce what the Latin-Americans call the 'chanfle'(a high curling shot that dips suddenly once over the wall). As a guide, always remember that it is just as impossible to approach the ball at full speed and then produce a perfectly placed swerving shot as it is to stand next to the ball and produce a powerfully drilled shot.

c) Also, there is more or less chance of conceding a goal from a 'free-kick' depending on where it is taken from. It might seem strange, but 'free-kick' specialists like Bebeto, Beckham, Rivaldo, Julinho, Suker or Pantic, are more likely to score a goal from 22 yards than from 17. The reason for this is perfectly logical. When the shot is swerved, the ball ascends and curls and once it passes the wall it dips towards the goal. If the shot is made close to the area, there is a good chance that if it has enough height to clear the wall that it will go over the crossbar, but if it is taken from 20-25 yards away the ball has enough time to drop and enter the goal.

d) Another interesting point: how many players should stand in the wall? Without doubt, this depends on the circumstances. If the 'free-kick' is directly opposite the goal then the wall should be made up of 5 players. However, if the goalkeeper knows that the player taking the 'free-kick' has a powerful shot (and he should know), he should add another player to the wall. But if the foul is to either side of the goal then he should remove 1-2 players, depending on how close the ball is to the wings. The further the ball is from the center, the fewer the number of players are needed in the wall. And so, if the 'free-kick' is taken at an angle near one of the wings, the wall will be made up of 2 players to avoid the ball being driven hard and low across the goal. Some goalkeepers put 7-8 players in the wall, which is not a good idea. This set -up reduces his visibility and if he wants to see the ball he has to stand near one of the posts. If the shot is then sent over the wall he has no chance of doing anything about it as he is too far away and a goal results. Also, with so many players in the wall, who marks the opposition and deals with the situation if the ball is played short as in a 'set move'?

e) Apart from the number of players in the wall, there are also a number of technical points to consider:

- If the goalkeeper knows (and he should) that the player taking the 'free-kick' has a powerful shot and likes to put swerve on the ball using the inside of his right foot, and if he has placed the wall to his right, (if the shot is fairly central), then he is better off placing the wall on the other side which will make it harder for the shooter. The goalkeeper must know (and should let his teammates know), that the ball is going to travel over the wall where the player number "4" is standing, if the 'marker' player is "1" and the player next to him is "2" etc. Therefore the goalkeeper must locate the tallest and bravest players in positions' "4" and "3", conscious of the fact that if they do not do a good job and/or the kicker is capable of placing ball over them (but close to them), it will go into the net. If it goes over the number "5", the goalkeeper will have a chance of reaching the ball; and if it goes over the other two players the ball will go wide of the post. Players' "3", "4" and "5", should jump as the kick is taken in an attempt to put the kicker off and/or block the shot. This action should be practiced repeatedly as it is not easy to achieve the necessary coordination so that the jump is timed perfectly to meet the ball.

- If the wall is set up at the other post, based on the same shooter, the two tallest players will act as the 'marker' and the player next to him where the goalkeeper knows that in order to score the striker has to kick the ball over them.

- This is also true for 'free-kick' specialists who use the outside of the foot, of which there are very few. Under these circumstances, the most appropriate position for the wall is to the right of the goalkeeper. He places the tallest players in the 'marker' area. If he places the wall on the other side, the positions would be identical to that mentioned for the shot with the inside of the foot but from the other side.

Also in a 2 or 3 player wall, if there is a rival who is a "chanfle" specialist (it does not matter whether he is going to center or shoot), the wall must be placed accordingly either to the right or to the left of the 'normal' position. But remember, often the foul is taken with the opposite foot. In other words, a left footer from the right and a right footer from the left. In both cases, moving the wall a yard towards the center of the field and with a tall player at the end, always makes it difficult for the shooter as the ball has to pass near the tallest player.

Finally it is incomprehensible to me that some goalkeepers let a teammate position himself close to the wall, perhaps a yard from it, usually so that he can run towards the ball. This position causes problems because not only does it reduce the goalkeeper's visibility but also the shot can be deflected by him, thus wrong-footing the goalkeeper and sending the ball to the far post instead of the near post (various goals have been scored in this way, including against the Spanish National team).

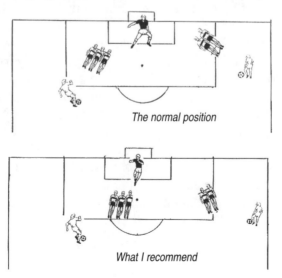

The normal position

What I recommend

The 'split' wall

f) The single wall is always talked about, but the "split" wall also exists. It was invented by the great Argentinean goalkeeper, Carrizo and it is particularly effective against the "chanfle" shot. The 'free-kick' specialists who use this technique agree that its success is not to do with the power in the shot but in finding the best area to place the ball.

The reason accuracy is more important than power is that the ball is placed on the opposite side of the goalkeeper and if the direction is right a goal is inevitable. On the other hand, if the goalkeeper places himself in the middle of the goal and sets up two walls of 3 players in each who cover both arcs, he will never be far away from the ball if it reaches the goal, and he will easily get to a weak but swerving shot. Furthermore, if the foul is to the side of the goal, one of the walls can be set up differently to the traditional ones. Perhaps this example will make this clearer. Suker is ready to play the 'free kick' with his left foot. The goalkeeper places the wall to the right of him in a classical fashion but the wall to the left he moves a yard further forwards, towards the other wall. He also puts the tallest and bravest player at the end of this wall, fully aware that if the ball is well struck it is likely to pass close to his head. There is very limited space on the other side and so if the ball goes there, the curl would send it out for a harmless goal-kick. Of course, this position is not appropriate for a right footer. In this case it would be necessary to move both the walls.

g) I want to make clear that I think the divided wall is usually the correct choice to make (if the shot is made from approximately 22 yards it is essential), if the opposition has a particularly good and skilful 'free-kick' specialist. However, if the shot is extremely powerful and well-directed then this type of wall is not effective at all. If the shot touches either of the players at the end of the walls, the ball can be deflected into the corners of the goal, leaving the goalkeeper powerless to do anything about it. Faced with this kind of shooter it is better to have one wall.

h) Many teams have an outfield player who organizes the team in these situations and he calls the attackers back to stand in the wall. This player decides on the wall and who should be in it. There is some logic in this:

- If the wall is formed using attackers, the defenders can concentrate on their job, which is marking.

- If there is a player responsible for the formation of the wall, the goalkeeper is free to concentrate on his own positioning and monitoring the opposition.

Nevertheless, I do not recommend it. The goalkeeper should position and form his own wall so that he is totally comfortable with it and he can exclusively concentrate on the player about to take the 'free-kick'. If the goalkeeper does not form his own wall and he is not happy with it then he will be so distracted that he will commit school-boy mistakes. Regarding who should stand in the wall, choose tall, brave players who play at the back, as this means that they are used to getting hit by the ball. I have often seen forwards placed in the wall get out of the way of the ball, worried about getting hit, leading to incredible but avoidable goals: A good example of this was Rayo vs Atletico Madrid in October '92. A powerfully struck 'free-kick' was taken by Garcia Cortes. Schuster and Manolo moved aside and a goal was scored.

The penalty is the most difficult thing for the goalkeeper to deal with, but the truth is that he has little to lose and much to gain. All the pressure is on the attacker as he is expected to score. In fact, even at the top level 25% of all penalties end in failure, i.e. one in every four. In other words goalkeepers are doing a good job (or perhaps the penalty takers a poor one). Saving penalties is often a natural gift, but it also depends on various other factors, of which experience and luck are very influential. Here are some recommendations that will help any goalkeeper improve his ability to save penalties:

During training sessions the goalkeeper should spend some time facing penalties, it does not matter who takes them. Even the Chairman of the club can take them if he likes. On average, face 10-15 shots from the 'ominous' spot and then analyze any thoughts, movements and also the penalty takers' techniques (if there are more than one). This type of practice should be done consistently on a regular basis so that as the years pass the goalkeeper will become more knowledgeable and experienced in dealing with this difficult situation.

Since the goalkeeper is never sure where the penalty taker is going to place the ball, it is a good idea to move slightly forwards before the shot is taken (this is illegal but all goalkeepers do it and the referees let them) but without committing himself too much. This makes the goal seem smaller and if the shot is not well aimed the goalkeeper has time to stop it.

It is also important to know as much about the penalty taker as possible: his strengths, his preferred technique and where he normally aims the ball. To help him with this, the goalkeeper should read the soccer newspapers and magazines and watch scrupulously on the TV how the best players take penalties.

THE 'INFALLIBLE' ZICO

Lots of strange psychology surrounds the penalty. If the penalty ends in goal, nobody recriminates the goalkeeper or praises the scorer. But if the goalkeeper stops the ball he is a hero and the penalty taker is heavily criticized.

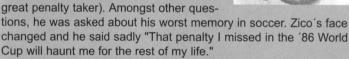

I recently saw the 'Great' Brazilian Zico, being interviewed on television (Zico was one of the best footballers of all time and a great penalty taker). Amongst other questions, he was asked about his worst memory in soccer. Zico´s face changed and he said sadly "That penalty I missed in the ´86 World Cup will haunt me for the rest of my life."

Indeed, Brazil were desperate to win the World Championship again (they hadn't won it since 1970), but they were eliminated when the infallible Zico missed a penalty. More than 15 years have passed and Zico still thinks about it and he always will.

LOOKING FOR PERFECTION

By this stage the goalkeeper has a very high standard and so it is advisable to try to improve and 'fine-tune' his skills on a daily basis. Perhaps it is a good idea to emphasize the point that above all, a good goalkeeper relies on intellect. So much so that probably no other player on the field has to use his 'soccer brain' as much as the goalkeeper. For this reason, the training needs to simulate 'real-match' situations as much as possible in order to develop this multi-tasking position as the goalkeeper needs to:

- See, sense and predict dangerous situations in advance.

- Have very quick reflexes to stop unexpected balls.

- Visualize and contain everything that is happening on the pitch (in his head), to initiate rapid counterattacks.

Unfortunately, even though the tactical planning and under-standing between the goalkeeper and the outfield players is a fundamental element in helping to create fast counterattacks, I know from experience that these are rarely practiced during train-ing. This is why I always recommend that all the training sessions are played under match conditions.

All players search for perfection. This is why I am going to give some advice to help achieve this goal:

1. Once the goalkeeper has reached a high level of competence, technical skills and moves should be carried out on all types of different pitch conditions (muddy, hard and slippery etc) and on a variety of surfaces. These are the factors which often deter-mine the level of the goalkeeper's success. There are, for example, goalkeepers who perform excellently on grass but struggle if they play on a hard pitch or on an artificial pitch because they are uncomfortable receiving the ball and are not happy diving for it.
How to deal with different conditions:

a) Dry surfaces facilitate a more technical and skilful game both in defense and in attack, although the goalkeeper can experience difficulties when diving on the hard pitch.

b) The opposite is true if the pitch is damp, as there is no problem diving but the game is less technical and defensive play in particular is very difficult (if there is a shot and the ball bounces on the 'greasy' pitch then it can go at such a speed that the goalkeeper has serious problems stopping it).

c) Grass pitches greatly benefit the goalkeeper in all aspects of the game.

d) Muddy pitches make technical moves and dives difficult as it is not easy to judge the pace of the ball and it can easily get stuck.

2. If you are lucky enough to train on an excellent grass pitch then I recommend that occasionally you train on a hard pitch. Also, the goalkeeper should take advantage of wet days (the ground could even be artificially watered) to train intensely and to familiarize himself with the difficulties that the wet surface creates. Also, if the goalkeeper knows that the next match will be played on a certain type of surface (very hard, muddy, slippery) then that week he should train on a ground under those same conditions.

3. Normally, a goalkeeper does not get involved very much in a game, but if the pitch size is smaller he has to intervene more often as there is hardly any space to develop the play: the ball goes from one end of the pitch to the other. Also, the goalkeeper has to deal with a lot more corners than usual, and even throw-ins near the goal cause problems. He will have to set up numerous walls during the match as even if his teammates commit fouls not too far from the center-circle there is a threat on goal because of the size of the pitch. As I have just said, if the goalkeeper knows he is going to play on this type of pitch then the coach should make sure that he has the opportunity to practice under these conditions the week before the

match.

4. One of the fundamental skills for the goalkeeper is good positioning. All goalkeepers must continue to learn this technique throughout their playing days, gaining expertise with experience.

Here is some advice about good positioning:

a) Outstanding goalkeepers are so used to running off their line to narrow the angle when an opponent is about to shoot that they do it automatically no matter what the circumstances or distances involved. If a player is about to shoot from 20-25 yards out, most goalkeepers move forward off their line. This is a mistake. It is better to stay near the goal, 40-50 inches in front of the goal-line, as even a high ball which is in the air for a relatively long time could suddenly dip and fly into the goal. If this happens, and the goalkeeper has come off his line the ball will go over his head into the back of the net. But on the other hand if he stays in the goal, even if the shot is well placed, given the distance of the shot he has time to move forward 2 or 3 steps and save it.

b) It is also a mistake to be caught off the goal-line when trying to save a header. These strikes on goal, except in exceptional cases, are never very powerful. For this reason it is better to stay in the goal when there is a header and to act once you see where it is going. Many goals are scored in this way: a moment before the shot the goalkeeper moves forward 2-3 yards, the strike is high because of the part of the body used, the goalkeeper does not get to the ball and the weak header goes into the goal. If the goalkeeper had stayed back he would have got to the ball easily.

c) It is essential to take short measured steps when getting into position. I remind you again that if the ball moves 1 yard either side of the pitch the goalkeeper should move approximately 15 inches in the same direction. On many occasions I have witnessed a forward receive the ball in front of the goal only to take it out wide, which is a bad move as it reduces his angle.

However, he shoots and scores at the far post for an obvious reason: the goalkeeper is poorly positioned because he moved too far towards the post nearest to the attacker. The only way to avoid this is to practice this move over and over.

5. I have already mentioned, but it is worth repeating again, that once the goalkeeper masters the dive he should not spend any time during training on specific diving exercises as this technique is rarely needed during a match. Nevertheless, even though it is used rarely it is still a vital and often decisive technique that merits a few pointers in this book:

a) During training, practice the technique used by the legendary Zamora. He always left more space on his favorite diving side when in a '1 v 1' in order to try to tempt the attacker into putting the ball there. If this move works for you in training then use it in matches.

b) Another move to try in the '1 v 1' is the move often used by the great Basque goalkeeper Iribar: the goalkeeper pretends to dive in one direction by moving his arms and body to that side as if anticipating the shot but instead he stays upright. Feints and dummies are often used by attackers but rarely performed by goalkeepers, though there is no logical explanation for this.

c) Another idea is to practice the technique used by the great

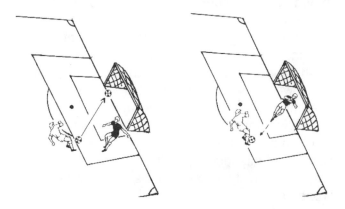

Positioning is fundamental

Catalan goalkeeper Ramallets when dealing with high curling shots. As the attacker was on the edge of the area ready to shoot, Ramallets would close him down and narrow the angle. The gifted attacker would nearly always try to widen the angle by putting swerve on the shot. The Catalan goalkeeper would always dive slightly backwards in order to be able to deflect the swerving ball clear of danger. If this very difficult technique works in training then use it in matches.

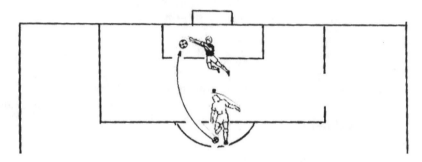

Ramallets and Kubala

Yashin's deflection

d) I have already mentioned that when the shot is close to the post the goalkeeper should deflect it with the hand nearest to it. Top quality goalkeepers use this technique when the shot is very low or at medium height but if faced by a high ball they deflect the ball using the hand furthest away from it (in other words, if the shot is going to their left, they dive to their left and save with their right hand). This is the correct technique to use as this allows the goalkeeper to totally extend his arm from the shoulder nearest the ball. This allows the goalkeeper to stretch further and increase his reach, making it a lot easier to get to the ball. The great Russian goalkeeper Yashin was a wonderful exponent of this technique. It was always a treat to watch him dive majestically to save the ball using what looked like the wrong hand.

6. In training, the goalkeeper should never just stay in goal facing

The goalkeeper makes contact with the ball with the palm of his hand to deflect it for a corner or send it along the by-line.

The goalkeeper should use his opposite hand when saving a high shot. This is the correct technique because it uses the shoulder closest to the ball. It also makes the shot seem longer.

his teammates' shots from the edge of the 18-yard box as this bears no resemblance to what happens during a match. This should only be done if one of the players in the team is exceptionally good at taking 'free-kicks' (as far as technique or power is concerned) where the goalkeeper uses this exercise to gain experience dealing with this technique. This helps the goalkeeper deal with a similarly gifted opponent during a match. Ramallets was able to perfect this technique thanks to his teammate Kubala. He went in goal and faced shot after shot from his gifted teammate, which after time gave him the experience and necessary know-how to familiarize himself to his teammate and this kind of technique.

7. All professional teams need to have a 'jet-ball' machine (or

similar automatic ball machine) to help them train. This machine benefits all the players but it is particularly useful for the goalkeeper: because the intensity of the shots can be regulated, swerve can be put on the ball and the goalkeeper does not waste any time as the shots are always efficient and accurate (for example, the only way to effectively practice the technique used by Ramallets i.e. dealing with swerving shots is to use the 'jetball'). A shrewd coach can also take advantage of the machine by using it in exercises that increase the goalkeeper's concentration and reflexes.

The goalkeeper can use the 'jet ball' machine for all sorts of exercises.

Once the goalkeeper has gained a good level of skill he needs to dedicate more time to the psychological side of the game. This is important for all soccer players but especially so for anyone playing in this position. Playing in goal requires a great deal of mental strength, will-power, patience, consistency, good concentration and awareness etc.

Goalkeepers should therefore dedicate plenty of time to training and relaxing the mind. I give good information about psychological and relaxing exercises in book 2 of my Spanish Coaching Bible in the chapter titled 'The Culmination - 19-30 years' which I thoroughly recommend you read. These exercises allow the player to improve motivation, relaxation, imagination, concentration and enable them to get in touch with their thoughts and feelings. Concentration is particularly important for the goalkeeper. He needs to dedicate a great deal of time to controlling and increasing his powers of concentration. This type of exercise can be done on the training pitch, in the changing rooms or at home (basically any time anywhere!).

This psychological training helps the goalkeeper deal with such things as being substitute enabling him to 'fight' for a place in the team and think positively. Only one goalkeeper can play in the team so even the top players have had to deal with being 'dropped' from time to time, which is sometimes difficult to take and often causes a great deal of mental stress and trauma.

The trajectory of outstanding goalkeepers is largely the same until they reach the highest level in the game: they are always the first-team choice as youngsters and receive nothing but plaudits. This continues through their teens. If they play for a 'big' club then they start in the reserve team or perhaps they play for a third division club. But sooner or later they move up to the 'first-team' where they experience being on the bench for the first time. Being a substitute is often too much of a trauma for some goalkeepers and they lose motivation and become depressed.

Of course this attitude is wrong! Being a substitute goalkeeper for the 'first-team' is not a tragedy! Accepting this situation with the correct attitude helps the goalkeeper develop a good temperament and professionalism. It also engenders other traits such as will-power, perseverance, tenacity and consistency. Goalkeepers such as Ramallets, Carmelo, Iribar and Arconada (all 'greats' in the game), all started off as substitutes and are good examples of what I have just said. The fact that they were not the 'first-team' choice made them work even harder. They learned all that they could from the more experienced players and sooner or later they all achieved their objectives and they went from strength to strength earning their place in the team.

I think that because the goalkeeper has such a psychologically demanding position, he particularly needs more technical and personal support from the coach. The goalkeeper needs to feel that the coach is taking a keen interest in what he does and that he can count on his support, admiration and friendship. If there are any coaches reading this let me tell you that it is up to you whether you have a good goalkeeper playing in your team or not.

If you continually use 'positive reinforcement' and praise, the goalkeeper gets the necessary motivation and contentment to go on to perform to his true potential. However, if you always criticize and show little confidence in him then this creates an indecisive, inconsistent and less motivated goalkeeper who will perform well below his best.

Van Gaal uses 'positive reinforcement' with his goalkeeper Hesp.

The 'Great' Zamora

The Catalan goalkeeper Ricardo Zamora is considered by many to be the best goalkeeper in the history of the game. He made his debut with Español at the age of 16 when he was still in shorts. And yet, due to his appearance, many people thought he had to be an experienced goalkeeper. He wore an English-style jersey with a high polo neck, gloves and a cap that was as hard as a crash helmet that kept the sun off his face and protected him from the knocks and bumps in the game. This protection was needed because in those days the goalkeeper could be 'wrestled' to the ground and generally 'man-handled' when he got the ball.

Because of this, he invented the 'Zamorano', which became famous throughout the world, and is now a topic of much debate among coaches as some feel it was an unnecessary move and that if any player uses it he will never be picked for the team. They seem to forget that today the circumstances in the game are totally different.

This is how the 'Great' goalkeeper explained the move to me many years ago: "The 'Zamorano' came about through fear, as an act of self-defense. In those days if you caught the ball the opposition was allowed to collide into you, push you over and knock you to your knees. If you fell over the goal-line a goal was awarded. At the age of 17 I was tall and skinny but not very strong and yet I had to play against sturdy and powerfully built experienced forwards aged around 25-28 years old and so I was always at a disadvantage. I came up with the idea that I could avoid the collisions by adopting the following tactic: when the ball came towards me with a couple of players in the opposition in hot pursuit, I did not try to catch the ball but instead I used to hit the ball clear with my arm and forearm which left them dis-orientated and chasing shadows."

This was a stroke of genius that not only helped the goalkeeper compensate for his physical inferiority but also made sure that he avoided the terrible clashes and collisions with the opposition that took a lot out of him physically. His great strength was his uncanny posi-tioning sense which allowed him to resolve a great many potentially difficult situations as he was always in the right place at the right time. The attackers in the opposition gave him a great deal of respect and the coaches told their players not to look at him or else it would be their downfall. This is how he got the name the 'Divino' (as it was thought that he could divine people's thoughts). For 20 years he was widely acclaimed as being the best goalkeeper in the world and he would have played a lot longer if it was not for the outbreak of the 'uncivil' war.

Do not think this is just my own personal bias and that I am exag-gerating. Recently I read the excellent book on goalkeeping 'Il portiere' by Bonizzoni and Laeli and in the chapter on the best goalkeepers of all time they say the following: "The best all round and most 'complete' goalkeeper who had the right combination of all the necessary skills (that no other player in the game has ever had) was the Spanish goal-keeper Zamora nicknamed the 'el Milagroso' (the Miracle Worker). Legend has it that he was even able to make the attackers place the ball where he wanted it to go. The ball always went straight to him. Zamora used feints and dummies to force the attacker to play the ball exactly where he wanted it. He had wonderful positioning sense plus a cat-like quality that allowed him to claim any ball. Other goalkeepers such as the Russian Yachin and the Spaniard Iribar played with a sim-ilar style, intuition and movement within the goal.

What else can I say?

Games and Exercises for Goalkeepers

No.	Objectives	Age	Developing the Games	Common Problems
1	Skills. Control over the ball and the body.	12-16	The goalkeeper performs various ball-juggling skills and passes the ball: between his legs, around his waist, around his neck, spins it on the tips of his fingers etc. This can be done to finish off the warm up.	The control with the fingers is poor. Some players get bored and do not want to do these exercises.
2	Skills. Control over the ball and the body. Acquiring the same technique as the outfield players.	14-16	The goalkeeper stands up straight with his hands stretched up above his head. He is holding a ball. He leans backwards and lets the ball drop, then he turns slightly and controls it with one of his feet (not letting the ball bounce). After 4-5 touches he catches the ball and places his arms behind his back. He then throws the ball up high over his head and controls it with his feet before it bounces. The goalkeeper earns a point each time he completes both parts correctly. Various goalkeepers can compete against each other and the one with the most points at the end wins.	These are two difficult movements that are not easy to perform correctly. Some goalkeepers become inhibited and make little progress if they cannot produce the moves correctly straight away.
3	Passing. Jumping. Skills. Using both hands.	14-16	2 goalkeepers stand 7 yards apart and take turns repeatedly passing high balls to each other. The balls are kicked to alternate sides (first to the left and then to the right). The goalkeeper has to catch the ball with his left hand (if the ball is on his left etc) and then throw it back to his partner using the same hand. Each time a player catches the ball and throws it back correctly he earns a point.	The balls are not kicked high enough. The players make no effort to move to reach an inaccurate pass. The players always try to use their preferred hand.

No.	Objectives	Age	Developing the Games	Common Problems
4	Jumping. Catching. Coordination. Controlling the space. Shouting - loudly and clearly (this is done during all the games and exercises).	14-16	A mini-trampoline and 3 goalkeepers. 1 of the goalkeepers is bouncing up and down on the trampoline and the other 2, each holding a ball, stand 6-8 yards away (one on each side). 1 player kicks his ball towards the one bouncing on the trampoline. The latter catches and immediately throws it back before turning, ready to receive the ball from the player on the other side. All the players swap and have a go on the trampoline and from each side of it.	The players do not time the jumps in order to bounce at the right height to receive the ball. Some players find it difficult to jump and turn at the same time.
5	Speed. Dexterity. Dribbling. Coordination. Determination to improve.	12-14	Two rows of 6 cones (each cone 2 yards apart) are parallel 4 yards apart. There are 2 goalkeepers (each holding a ball) at the end of each row. On the signal 1 player from each team starts bouncing the ball around the cone obstacle course using both hands as quickly as possible. When the player finishes the course he heads the ball to the player waiting. The fastest pairing earns a point. After these have finished the other teams have a go. The team with the most points wins.	The teams are not always well-matched (this ruins the game). The players bounce the ball, catch it and then bounce it again. The ball should be bounced continuously and never caught. The players do not head the ball to the next player.

Fig 3

Fig 5

No.	Objectives	Age	Developing the Games	Common Problems
6	Speed. Dribbling. Changing pace and direction. Coordination. Dexterity.	12-14	3 cones, 8 yards apart, form a triangle. 6 other cones (1 yard apart) are placed between 2 of these cones. There are 3 goal-keepers on each of the other sides. On the signal a player from each team sets off bouncing the ball around the cones. This takes place around the outside of the cones and in and out on the side where there are lots of cones. Once the player gets back to where he started he heads the ball to the next player and he has a turn and so on. The quickest team around the cones earns 1 point. The team with the most points at the end wins.	The teams are not always well-matched (this ruins the game). The players bounce the ball, catch it and then bounce it again. The ball should be bounced con-tinuously and never caught. The players do not head the ball to the next play-er. The players find it diffi-cult to change pace.

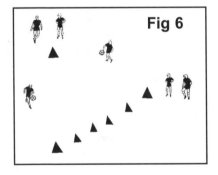

Fig 6

No.	Objectives	Age	Developing the Games	Common Problems
7	Speed. Changing pace and direction. Feints and dummies. Dribbling. Focused and peripheral vision. Dexterity.	14-16	Pitch size 20 x 20y. 6 goalkeepers each carrying a ball and 2 are also carrying a bib. On the signal, all the players start bouncing the ball, keeping an eye on where all the other players are located. The 2 players with a bib have to try to 'tag' any of the others in order to swap roles. The players try to avoid getting 'tagged' by playing feints and dummies, changing pace and direction suddenly. Never-ending duels should be avoided. No matter what the outcome, whether the player is 'tagged' or not, after the challenge a new player is sought.	Some goalkeepers stop and look around. There should be constant movement. Always chasing the same player. Some players do not look up.
8	Quick reflexes. Speed. Anticipation. (The best age to improve reaction speed is between 10-20).	14-16	2 goalkeepers stand close together on the goal line. The coach stands on the 6-yard line holding a ball up high in each hand with his arms extended. Suddenly he lets a ball drop and the goalkeepers have to sprint off the line in an attempt to catch the ball before it bounces. This is repeated several times but with a long break in between attempts so that the players are always fully rested before trying again.	The players do not sprint and dive and so rarely get to the ball in time. The goalkeepers impede each other so much that neither of them get to the ball in time before it bounces.

Fig 7

Fig 8

No.	Objectives	Age	Developing the Games	Common Problems
9	Quick reflexes. Speed. Jumping. Anticipation. Punching.	15-16	2 goalkeepers standing close together on the goal line with their backs to the coach who stands on the 6-yard box holding a ball. The coach bounces the ball hard and as soon as the players hear this they turn, rush out, and jump to claim the ball. They can also punch the ball away. This is repeated several times but with a long break in between attempts so that the players are fully rested before trying again.	Sometimes a goalkeeper gets to the ball slightly before the other but as he tries to claim the ball the latter punches it away.
10	Quick reflexes. Focused vision. Special speed.	14-16	2 goalkeepers are standing 15 yards apart. 1 of the players is holding a tennis ball. The ball is thrown as hard as possible towards the other player who has to use one hand (left or right alternately) to try to catch it. Then the roles are reversed, the player with the ball throws it back to the other player who has to try to catch it. This game becomes even more difficult as the players get slightly closer after each throw until they are only 5 yards apart. Each successful catch earns 1 point. The player with the most points at the end wins.	When the players are close together they do not throw the ball hard enough. The ball is thrown to the wrong hand. The exercises are done one after the other when the coach should make sure that the players have enough rest.

No.	Objectives	Age	Developing the Games	Common Problems
11	Quick reflexes. Focused vision. Special speed. Twists and turns.	14-16	A goalkeeper stands close to a wall (in front of it). Another player stands behind him and throws tennis balls at the wall from different heights and angles. The goalkeeper tries to catch each ball in one hand. Both players frequently swap roles. When the players get used to the game, to make things more difficult, the goalkeeper stands with his back to the wall and has to turn before catching the ball. The 2 players can compete against each other.	The ball is thrown at the same height and from the same distance. These should always be varied. The balls are not thrown hard enough. The players do not take enough rest in between games.
12	Quick reflexes. Focused and peripheral vision. Anticipation. Catching. Twists and turns.	14-16	A goalkeeper stands in front of a wall (facing it). Another player stands behind him and kicks a ball against the wall from both sides. The goalkeeper has to react quickly and anticipate the direction the ball is coming from. The players swap roles regularly. After a while the goalkeeper faces the kicker and so has to turn before attempting to catch the ball. As the players get older they use a wall with an uneven surface so that the rebound is less predictable.	Lack of concentration. The goalkeepers wait for the ball to come to them (if it is rebounding towards them). This is a serious mistake that needs to be corrected. The players do not take enough rest in between games.

Fig 12

No.	Objectives	Age	Developing the Games	Common Problems
13	Quick reflexes. Focused and peripheral vision. Anticipation.	15-16	The goalkeeper stands in front of two walls that are next to each other (a gymnasium wall could be used instead). A player behind him kicks a ball against one of the walls, always varying the angle. As soon as the goalkeeper sees the ball rebound he tries to block it or intercept it before it bounces. Both players change roles at regular intervals.	Lack of concentration. Not running towards the ball. The players do not take enough rest in between games.
14	Paying attention. Concentration. Positioning.	13-15	The coach stands on the penalty spot with a ball at his feet. The goalkeeper stands on the edge of the six-yard box in the classic position (knees bent, arms away from the body and slightly leaning forward). The coach approaches the goal from different angles (from each wing to the middle of the pitch). The coach always tells the goalkeeper if his positioning is correct and on occasion will shoot at goal. The goalkeeper should adjust his position by taking very small movements, by dragging his feet almost without lifting them off the ground. This is a very physically demanding exercise and so various goalkeepers rotate at regular periods.	Poor positioning. The goalkeeper usually stands too close to the post nearest the ball. The goalkeeper is in the correct position but dives before the coach kicks the ball.

Fig 14

No.	Objectives	Age	Developing the Games	Common Problems
15	Paying attention. Concentration. Positioning.	14-16	The goalkeeper stands in goal and there are 4 balls spaced out in the 18-yard box. The goalkeeper is fully aware that each ball has been given a number. If for example the coach calls out 'number 3' then the goalkeeper positions himself correctly in between the posts and the ball as he moves to narrow the angle. Suddenly the coach calls out another number and the goalkeeper takes up a different position. This is done until all 4 balls have been used. The coach then changes the location of the balls. Then another goalkeeper has a turn. A goalkeeper earns a point each time he takes up a correct position. The player with the most points at the end wins.	It is very difficult to expect perfect positioning. This requires a lot of soccer knowledge and experience plus a tremendous level of concentration.

Fig 15

Fig 17

No.	Objectives	Age	Developing the Games	Common Problems
16	Correct technique for running sideways. Diving to the left or right.	14-16	Once the goalkeepers are used to diving to the left or to the right, they practice running sideways. A goalkeeper stands on the goal-line much closer to one post than the other. The coach or another player kicks a ball towards the big gap and the goalkeeper has to run sideways to save the ball. The goalkeeper should dive for the ball after taking 3 steps to the side. Some goalkeepers will find that they only need to make two strides before the dive (each goalkeeper should do whatever he is comfortable with). The goalkeeper must leave enough space to his left or right for the dive.	Poor positioning of the feet (they should be pointing in the direction of the ball). Instead of moving for the ball the goalkeeper uses his hand to help soften his landing. Goalkeepers sometimes try to gather the ball when pushing it out for a corner is the best option. Some goalkeepers feel discomfort when diving (the hips should be at an angle of 90° to the ground).
17	Punching technique when challenged by an opponent. Coordination. Dominating the space.	15-16	The goalkeepers are spread around the pitch in groups of 3. One of the players has a ball and the two are 8-10 yards away from him (but close to each other) playing the roles of goalkeeper and attacker. The player with the ball kicks it up high towards the other two players. The goalkeeper tries to punch the ball as far away as possible while being harassed (not excessively) by the player acting as the attacker. The three player swap in order to experience each role. A point is awarded each time the goalkeeper makes an effective punch.	The big mistake is to make contact with the ball with the arm fully extended. The elbow is extended after contact has been made with the ball (all the energy projected through the elbow should be utilized as contact is made).

No.	Objectives	Age	Developing the Games	Common Problems
18	Jumping. Heading. Bravery. Reflexes. Agility.	15-16	A 'round' played in an area 20 x 20 yards. 2 goalkeepers are inside standing shoulder to shoulder and there are 4 other goalkeepers standing outside this area. One of the players on the outside throws in a ball which the 2 players inside the area jump to try to head. After the header the players inside have to stay alert and save various balls coming from any direction, speed and height. These shots end when one of the goalkeepers is able to gather the ball or if the ball is kicked far away (if the balls are parried the game continues). Once the shooting has finished 2 of the players on the outside take a turn jumping for the header and saving the ball. Then the third pairing go into the middle and so on.	Poor positioning before the jump. Not reacting quickly enough after the jump to save the balls. The players on the outside do not kick the ball hard enough. The players in the middle try to stop the balls calmly (this should be done as fast as possible).

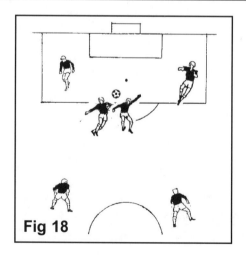

Fig 18

No.	Objectives	Age	Developing the Games	Common Problems
19	Jumping. Heading. Controlling the goalmouth area.	14-16	Pitch size 12 x 8 yards. 8 players: a goalkeeper in each goal (7 a-side goals) and 2 outfield players per team. There is a 'neutral' player on each wing. These players always help the team on the ball. The goalkeepers are expected to help by shouting instructions to the outfield players. If a simple ball arrives, the goalkeepers should head it and if possible towards a 'neutral' player. If a goalkeeper gathers the ball or a goal-kick is awarded he passes the ball to the opposition's half by way of a jumping header.	Easy balls are often caught when a header is required. The goalkeepers make little effort to dive in order to save a ball heading for goal near one of the posts.
20	Balance. Coordination. Spatial orientation after a forward roll. Jumping.	13-15	3 goalkeepers form a triangle. 2 of the goalkeepers have a ball and the third waits to spring into action. On the signal this player does a forward roll and as he gets back into position he jumps to save a ball that is thrown up for him (he never knows which of the 2 players is going to throw the ball up for him). Then the other players take a turn.	Repeating this type of exercise helps those players who suffer from a mild form of vertigo or poor balance.

Fig 20

No.	Objectives	Age	Developing the Games	Common Problems
21	Balance. Coordination. Spatial orientation. Jumping.	14-16	3 goalkeepers are in a line 2 yards apart bouncing a ball each on the run. On the signal the players stop running and immediately drop their ball. Once the balls have bounced the goalkeepers dive to their right to claim one. They immediately produce a forward roll (without letting go of the ball), get back into line and each player throws his ball up high and jumps up to catch it. The exercise continues in this way with the appropriate rest periods.	The player furthest right has to run and collect the ball from the player furthest left, which is not easy. Some players lose orientation when performing the above maneuver.

Fig 21

No.	Objectives	Age	Developing the Games	Common Problems
22	Balance. Coordination. Spatial orientation. 'Throwing' yourself at the ball.	15-16	6 goalkeepers. 1 in goal and the other 5 positioned near the penalty spot. The coach is next to one of the goal-posts with several balls at his feet. On the signal one of the players advances towards the goal. On the next signal the goalkeeper and advancing player perform a forward roll. As they get to their feet the coach throws up a ball for the advancing player to produce a diving header. The goalkeeper tries to avoid conceding a goal. The player who produced the diving header now goes in goal and another player advances and so on until each of the 6 goalkeepers have had a turn experiencing both roles.	Some players experience a mild form of vertigo or disorientation but this soon passes.

Fig 22

Fig 23

No.	Objectives	Age	Developing the Games	Common Problems
23	The goal-kick (maximum acceleration with the kicking foot). Improvisation. Dominating the goalmouth area. Throwing the ball out. (if there are not enough goalkeepers for this game then outfield players or the coaching staff help out).	15-16	6 goalkeepers. 2 players practice taking goal-kicks (from both sides of the pitch). 2 players with various balls are positioned a few yards beyond the 18-yard box (one on the left and one on the right). The other 2 players are separated in the same way near the halfway line. On the signal, one of the goalkeepers takes a goal-kick, sending the ball to one of the players near the halfway line. If the goal-kick is not good (poor direction or lacking the necessary power) the player on the other side of the halfway line comes across and shoots at goal as hard as he can. The goalkeeper who took the poor goal-kick positions himself correctly so that he can save the shot. If he is successful he throws the ball to the player on the halfway line who should have received it earlier from the goal-kick. If the throw is powerful and accurate enough no shot is taken. The 2 goalkeepers swap sides and take turns taking the goal-kicks. All the players rotate in order to experience each role.	Poor goal-kicks. Poor contact made with the ball. The goalkeepers take too long to reposition themselves in order to save the shots after a poor goal-kick. They forget to throw the ball out.

No.	Objectives	Age	Developing the Games	Common Problems
24	Quick reflexes. Acceleration. Taking goal-kicks quickly.	14-16	3 goalkeepers (one holding a ball) stand very close together. The 2 without the ball jog side by side. The player with the ball volleys it over their heads from behind them. As the two players spot the ball they run forward and dive to catch it before it bounces. The pass needs to be high and accurate, placed 4-5 yards in front of the players. The player who gets to the ball immediately throws it back to the player who made the pass. All the players swap roles.	Some goalkeepers are too slow to react. Some are afraid to dive for the ball (this should be practiced at the 'suspended' ball). The players forget to throw the ball back. Inaccurate volleys.
25	Diving forwards. Running backwards. Kicking and throwing the ball out. 'Special' speed.	15-16	Various goalkeepers in goal intervene alternately. The coach stands on the edge of the 18-yard box with various balls. He throws a ball up high towards the penalty spot. The goalkeeper sprints and dives forwards to collect the ball and then immediately throws it out to the player waiting on the halfway line. The goalkeeper then runs backwards towards the goal as the coach throws up another ball for him. If the goalkeeper manages to save this ball he immediately kicks it out towards the player waiting on the halfway line. As the goalkeeper kicks the ball one of the other goalkeepers acts as the 'fly'. The 'fly' is the term used for the player who harasses and obscures the vision of the player trying to perform a certain task.	At this age the players find it very difficult to run backwards. The players find kicking the ball out a problem. (this is due to lack of experience and often the player forgets to kick the ball out). The goalkeepers find it difficult to overcome the 'fly'. (they should run with the ball to make the necessary space).

No.	Objectives	Age	Developing the Games	Common Problems
26	Positioning. 'Hold' position and time the intervention. Reading the play. Throwing the ball out.	14-16	Various goalkeepers in the goal intervene alternately. Various players (with a ball each) are positioned on the edge of the 18-yard box. On the signal, one of these players runs towards the goal and a '1 v 1' confrontation develops. The goalkeeper, with knees bent, holds his position and waits for the best moment to try to gather the ball. If he is successful he immediately throws the ball out to the member of the coaching staff who called for the ball. After two interventions the next goalkeeper has a turn. The coach gives feedback on the positive and negative aspects of the play.	Some coaches make their best players act as strikers which demoralizes the goalkeepers (less gifted players should be used at first and then introduce the better players at a later date). Some strikers shoot. These players need to try again and be reminded that they have to dribble.
27	Positioning. 'Hold' position and time the intervention. Reading the game. Anticipation. Throwing the ball out.	15-16	A 'round' 18 x 18 yards. 6 goalkeepers. 2 inside the area and 4 outside (these have a ball each). 2 players on the outside enter the area with a ball each to start 2 '1 v 1' confrontations. If the striker gets past the goalkeeper he goes back outside the area. If a player in the middle manages to gather the ball he immediately throws it out to one of the coaching staff who called for it. Either way, the other two players enter the area to try to beat the goalkeepers. The players swap in order to experience each role.	The goalkeepers sometimes try to win the ball immediately and do not wait until the time is right. The players forget to throw the ball out.

No.	Objectives	Age	Developing the Games	Common Problems
28	Passing. Making space. Dribbling. Getting a 'feel' for the game. Reading the game. Diving.	12-14	2 players (one with a ball) are 6-8 yards apart. There is a goalkeeper in between them. The idea of the game is for the strikers to pass the ball to each other while the goalkeeper tries to intercept it. The game involves diving, passing the ball into the 'light' and dribbling etc. This is a very tiring game, especially for the player in the middle and so the players swap regularly and there are numerous rest periods.	Not passing the ball into the 'light'. The goalkeeper never anticipates what the strikers are going to do. Not diving quickly enough.

Fig 27

No.	Objectives	Age	Developing the Games	Common Problems
29	Positioning (the goalkeepers should remain in the center of the circle). Catching. Diving. Deflections.	13-15	3 goalkeepers play alternately. 6-8 players form a 'round' with a diameter of 20 yards. The goalkeeper is in the middle and it is his job to try to deflect, intercept or catch the ball as it is passed across between the players (the players can also pass to each other outside the area). The passes have to be along the ground, at medium height or at most a yard above the goalkeeper's head. This is a tiring game for the goalkeeper so they swap regularly.	The goalkeeper does not stay in the center. If the goalkeeper fails to hold onto the ball he recovers slowly and is not ready for the next intervention.
30	Passing. Reading the game. Analyzing the opposition. Diving. Anticipation.	15-16	A 'round' similar to the previous game. 6 players on the outside and 2 goalkeepers in the middle (2 other goalkeepers wait to swap in). The strikers pass the ball to each other taking a maximum of two touches. The goalkeepers try to intercept the ball. If they touch the ball but fail to hold onto it, play continues. If a goalkeeper manages to get hold of the ball he immediately throws it to the other 2 goalkeepers jogging near the halfway line waiting their turn. This is a tiring game and so the goalkeepers swap regularly.	The strikers do not make any risky passes, which gives the goalkeepers little chance of winning the ball. The goalkeepers do not anticipate well. The goalkeeper fails to throw it out when he gets the ball.

No.	Objectives	Age	Developing the Games	Common Problems
31	Concentration. Focused and peripheral vision. Passing ability. Improvisation. Reading the game. Diving to intercept the passes.	14-16	A 'round' similar to the previous game. 6 players on the outside and 2 goalkeepers in the middle (2 other goalkeepers jog near the halfway line waiting to swap in). Ideally, the strikers should also be goalkeepers (or as many as possible). The game is played using hands and a tennis ball. The ball is passed between the players on the outside and they have to catch it one-handed. The goalkeepers in the middle try to intercept the ball. If one of the goalkeepers in the middle touches the ball but fails to catch it then one of the players on the outside can enter the area momentarily to retrieve the ball. Any player who drops the ball or has it intercepted swaps with the player who has been in the middle the longest. The player with the ball cannot move as those looking to receive it make space and get into a catching position.	The 2 players in the middle should work together but they rarely do. Lots of balls are dropped. Any player who passes the ball along the ground or too high in the air is penalized and has to go in the middle.

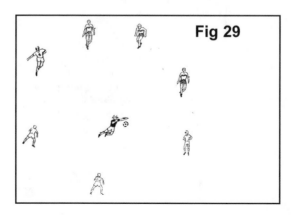

Fig 29

No.	Objectives	Age	Developing the Games	Common Problems
32	Playing in goal. Organizing the team. Quick distribution (seeing what is on). Developing the role as an outfield player.	12-13	A '5-a-side' game is played in an appropriate area. Goals are 7 x 21'. The goalkeepers play as usual but the coach is making sure that they: 1.Organize the team by constantly shouting instructions. 2.Release the ball quickly before the opposition has a chance to re-organize. Sometimes, the goalkeeper plays as an outfield player for a short period of time.	Not organizing the other players. Shouting poor instructions. Distributing the ball too slowly. Releasing the ball quickly but with little accuracy. The idea is to achieve speed and accuracy.
33	Getting a 'feel' for the game (as a goalkeeper and as an outfield player). Understanding and starting the moves in 'the method'. Being an 'all round' goalkeeper.	12-14	Pitch size 30 x 20 yards. Goals 7 x 21'. This is a game of '3 v 3'. The team without the ball plays with a goalkeeper while the attacking team use all 3 players to practice the moves in 'the method' and to take advantage of numerical superiority. No counterattack is allowed when the defending team wins the ball. Instead, there is a stop in play as the now defending team positions a player in goal and all 3 players in the attacking team get ready to play the moves in 'the method' in the hope of scoring a goal. In this way, the goalkeepers play in goal when the team is defending and they join in the attack when the team is on the offensive. If the goalkeeper gets the ball he immediately passes it to the coach who puts it back in play once the two teams have re-organized.	The goalkeepers find it difficult to adapt to the change of role. The defenders stay in the central area of the pitch or drop right back to the goal. This has to be corrected or else the objectives of the game will never be achieved.

No.	Objectives	Age	Developing the Games	Common Problems
34	Playing in goal. Throwing the ball (power and accuracy).	14-16	2 '7 a-side' goals measuring 7 x 21' are positioned 15 yards apart. 2 goalkeepers alternate in each goal. One of the goalkeepers has a ball and the idea is to score a goal by throwing it past the other goalkeeper into the net opposite. The goalkeeper who scores the most goals is the winner.	Some players get closer to the goal before throwing he ball. This is not allowed as they must throw the ball from the goal-line. However, a run up is permitted.
35	Playing in goal. Shooting (power and accuracy).	14-16	Two goals 7 x 21' with a goalkeeper in each. Similar to the previous game except: 1.The distance between the goals is 30 yards. 2.The ball is kicked. 3.The player can run with the ball to the halfway line before shooting. The player who scores the most goals is the winner. It is important that the coach keeps a tally of the goals scored and conceded.	Some players shoot from distance when they are allowed to run up to the halfway line. Some shoot without taking a run-up and so the strike lacks power. Poor technique. This is practiced at the 'suspended' ball if necessary.

Fig 33

Fig 34

No.	Objectives	Age	Developing the Games	Common Problems
36	Anticipation. Reading the game. Passing. Jumping. Coordination. Controlling the space around you.	14-16	This is a game of '2 v 2' using a basketball hoop which is the same for both teams. The ball cannot be bounced and the idea is to shoot as often as possible. The players should pay particular attention to claiming the ball if it rebounds. If the defending team claim the ball then the game is restarted from the shooting zone.	The ball is bounced. Making little effort to claim the ball from rebounds. Defenders do not wait to re-start the game from the shooting zone if they win the ball.
37	Teamwork. Short and long passing. Improving catching. Using feet. Intuition for knowing which goal to go to.	14-16	This game is '5 v 5' using half a regulation size pitch. In total four goals are used, the regulation size goal, one on each wing and one on the halfway line. The rules are as follows: 1.Maximum 'three-touch'. 2.Both teams try to keep possession by playing a series of short and medium length passes. 3.The goalkeepers (one in each team) have to defend all four goals. 4.A point is scored each time a team plays a long high pass to its goalkeeper and he catches it safely. The goalkeeper then places the ball on the ground and passes it to a teammate and the process begins again. The long passes cannot be made to the same goal twice in a row. The team with the most points at the end wins.	Short passes are made to the goalkeeper. These have to be long passes. The goalkeepers do not 'read' the game and help the team by going to a goal where the ball is most likely to go.

No.	Objectives	Age	Developing the Games	Common Problems
38	Perfecting the system of play. Organizing the team. Improvisation. Intelligence. Reading the game.	14-16	This game is '7-a-side' using half a regulation size pitch. The outfield players practice the moves in 'the method' and the goalkeepers shout instructions and organize the team ("the players at the back help the players further forward"). There is a 'wall' next to each post. If the ball rebounds off them the game continues. This makes it difficult for the goalkeepers, especially if a striker uses the 'walls' intelligently and intentionally plays to get the rebound.	The goalkeepers either do not try to organize their teammates or if they do, they shout poor instructions. The players do not take advantage of the 'walls'.
39	Perfecting the system of play. Spatial awareness. Peripheral vision. Organizing the team.	15-16	This game is '7-a-side' using half a regulation size pitch. The goals are only one yard wide and the goalkeepers play as outfield players all over the pitch. When the other team has the ball the goalkeeper can intercept it using his hands (anywhere on the pitch)but he is not allowed to hold onto it. The team that scores the most goals wins.	The temptation is too great and sometimes the goalkeepers touch the ball with their hands when they are attacking. Some goalkeepers do not stray far from their goal. They have to be encouraged to roam freely throughout the whole pitch.

No.	Objectives	Age	Developing the Games	Common Problems
40	Perfecting the system of play. Spatial awareness. Peripheral vision. Organizing the team.	16-18	This game is '7-a-side' using half a regulation size pitch played width-ways. The goals are marked by cones on what are normally the wings. The players practice the moves in 'the method'. The goalkeepers are expected to organize the rest of the team. Form time to time, to improve spatial awareness, the coach will move the goals a few yards left or right. The coach is keen to see how the players (especially the goalkeeper) react to the change. Players have to see that the goals have been moved and they are not allowed to alert team-mates although they themselves can take full advantage of the new circumstances.	Some players demonstrate poor spatial awareness. Players spend their time waiting for the goals to be changed and fail to play the moves in 'the method'. Some goalkeepers organize the team well while others have little idea.
41	Ball skills. Controlling both body and ball. Acquiring the same skills as outfield players.	16-18	Each goalkeeper is holding a ball. The goalkeeper throws the ball up high and tries to catch it behind his back. Then the ball is thrown up again and the goalkeeper gets back to his starting position. When this is mastered the goalkeeper starts to develop skills using his feet as follows: The ball is thrown up and then kept up a few times using both feet before it is kicked up and caught behind the back. This exercise is repeated and a point is awarded each time it is done successfully.	Some goalkeepers find it difficult to complete the second half of the exercise (using the feet). They should keep trying and never give up.

No.	Objectives	Age	Developing the Games	Common Problems
42	Ball skills. Focused and peripheral vision. Paying attention. Concentration. Technique - eyes, hands and feet. Jumping.	17-18	The goalkeepers are put in pairs. One is carrying a ball and the other has a ball at his feet. The players are 6-8 yards apart. The balls are passed at the same time, one in the air and one along the ground. One goalkeeper catches the ball and immediately throws it back while the other player kicks the ball back 'first-time'. Once this is mastered the players throw the ball up high so that they have to jump to catch it (the pass with the feet remains the same).	Some goalkeepers find it difficult to concentrate on both balls at the same time. Others adapt immediately without any problems.

Fig 41

Fig 42

No.	Objectives	Age	Developing the Games	Common Problems
43	Paying attention. Concentration. Ability to make quick decisions. Explosive power. Agility. Acceleration. Releasing the ball quickly.	17-18	This exercise involves 3 goalkeepers. One goalkeeper is in goal and the other two are located on the edge of the 18-yard box. These goalkeepers kick a ball each (one towards one post and one towards the other). The goalkeeper saves one shot and then tries to scramble across to save the other. If he manages to save the second ball, he throws it out to one of players. The goalkeepers swap roles on a regular basis.	It is difficult to concentrate on both balls at the same time. The goalkeepers find it difficult to know which ball to save first. They forget to throw the ball out at the end.
44	Paying attention. Concentration. Quick reflexes. Agility. Releasing the ball quickly.	17-18	This exercise involves 3 goalkeepers. One goalkeeper stands on the goal line facing the net. The coach stands on the edge of the 18-yard box. As he shoots the ball he shouts out a number. If the goalkeeper hears 1, 5 or 7 he turns to save the ball. If any other number is called out the goalkeeper does not move. A note is made of each time the goalkeeper reacts correctly to the signal. Once the shot has been taken another goalkeeper acts as the 'fly' and takes advantage of any rebound. If the goalkeeper saves the ball he releases it by kicking it out while being impeded and harassed by the 'fly'.	Difficult to concentrate. The goalkeepers turn around when they should not and they react slowly to a bona fide signal. If a goalkeeper fails to hold on to a shot he makes little effort to stop the 'fly' scoring from the rebound.

No.	Objectives	Age	Developing the Games	Common Problems
45	Paying attention. Concentration. Quick reflexes. Acceleration. Speed. Diving forwards. Releasing the ball quickly.	17-18	8 players. One stands on the goal line and the other on the edge of the 18-yard box. A player stands on each side of the 18-yard box and four players wait to swap in. The idea of the game is that a ball is positioned in the center of the area and on the signal the players run forwards and dive to claim the ball. The player who manages to claim the ball immediately throws it to a position indicated by the coach. All the goalkeepers swap positions and the game restarts. The goalkeepers waiting swap at regular intervals and all the players experience the game from each starting point as the distance varies from 8 to 20 yards.	Goalkeepers rarely dive forwards in the modern game as they invariably use their feet. It is a very useful technique that requires bravery and plenty of practice. Not all the goalkeepers run at a similar speed. To compensate for speed or lack of speed some goalkeepers should always sprint from the goal line (shorter distance) and some from the edge of the 18-yard box (greater distance).

Fig 43

No.	Objectives	Age	Developing the Games	Common Problems
46	Paying attention. Concentration. Quick reflexes. Bravery. Orientation. Dominating the space around you. Explosive power. Acceleration. Diving. Releasing the ball quickly.	17-18	A number of goalkeepers are split into pairs and take turns doing the following exercise: The first two players (the others wait their turn) are lying face down next to each other with their eyes shut (they are so close that they are touching). They know that the coach is positioning a ball somewhere approximately 5 yards away. When ready, the coach gives a signal or touches both players simultaneously and they both jump up, locate the ball and try to claim it by diving on it. The player who claims the ball immediately throws it to one of the waiting goalkeepers. Then the next pairing has a go and so on. The appropriate rest periods are taken as required.	The goalkeepers find the orientation difficult and take time to adapt. Lack of determination and bravery when trying to claim the ball. Forgetting to throw the ball at the end.
47	Out-jumping an adversary. Punching (power and accuracy). Coordination. Anticipation. Dominating the space around you.	17-18	The goalkeepers are put into groups of three (of similar height and ability). One of the goalkeepers is holding a ball and the other two are jogging 15 yards away from him. The ball is thrown up and the two players jump, trying to punch it clear (with power and direction). The players continually swap roles.	Some goalkeepers jump when they are nowhere near the ball. Some find it difficult to get used to the proximity of the other goalkeeper. Poor coordination as far as contact with the ball and elbow extension are concerned.

No.	Objectives	Age	Developing the Games	Common Problems
48	Dealing with crosses. Punching. '1 v 1'. Releasing the ball quickly. Concentration.	18-20	9 players. 2 (1 at each corner) ready to cross the ball. 3 goalkeepers in the middle acting as strikers. 3 players stand 10 yards beyond the 18-yard box. A goalkeeper on the goal line ready to clear the danger. A ball is crossed and the goalkeeper tries to punch it clear towards the center of the pitch. If the ball clears these attackers then a cross is taken from the other corner. If the clearance goes to one of these players waiting beyond the 18-yard box then he runs forward and challenges the goalkeeper in a '1 v 1' confrontation. If the goalkeeper claims the ball he immediately throws it to the other corner so that it can be crossed back in from this side of the pitch. The goalkeepers swap roles regularly and so do the outfield players. A point is earned for each clearance that goes beyond the 3 players and for each ball claimed during the '1 v 1'.	The crosses should be at the appropriate height but they are not always well-executed. The punching technique is often poor. The player who advances with the ball for the '1 v 1' shoots when he has to try to dribble around the goalkeeper.

Fig 46

Fig 47

No.	Objectives	Age	Developing the Games	Common Problems
49	Paying attention. Concentration. Positioning. Orientation.	17-18	Various goalkeepers alternate. A goalkeeper is in goal and 2 attackers are in the penalty area 10-12 yards apart passing a ball to each other. The goalkeeper positions himself correctly between the ball and the goal as the former is passed from side to side. If the strikers see that the goalkeeper is poorly positioned they shoot. The coach stands in the goal to monitor the goalkeeper's positioning and movements. From time to time, the coach will signal for a shot to be taken, which he expects the goalkeeper to save, to confirm he is positioned correctly. The 'fly' looks to pounce if the goalkeeper spills the ball and if not he harasses him when he tries to kick it up field. As always the goalkeepers swap roles regularly.	Poor positioning. The goalkeeper is in the correct position but he dives and commits himself before the striker shoots. Some goalkeepers lose their temper with the 'fly' as he impedes the clearance.

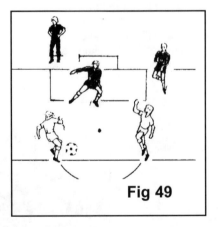

Fig 49

No.	Objectives	Age	Developing the Games	Common Problems
50	Paying attention. Concentration. Positioning. Orientation. Dribbling. Feints and dummies. Speed of execution. Long passing.	18-20	This is a similar game to the previous one but it is more complicated. Apart from the positioning, shooting and volleyed clearances, the coach (who is always standing behind the goalkeeper) gives a signal for the striker on the ball to pass it using the inside of the foot to the goalkeeper and then sprint after it to try to win it back. The goalkeeper has to try to play the ball out of the 18-yard box while being pressured by the 'fly' (he does not try too hard), the striker who passed the ball and the other striker who has also sprinted after the ball. If the goalkeeper is successful he passes the ball to a coach or player waiting near the middle of the pitch. If the goalkeeper loses the ball then with the help of the 'fly' he tries to win the ball back. The strikers show no mercy and score if they get the chance. The goalkeepers swap regularly.	It is important for the strikers to be genuine attacking players so that the goalkeeper experiences a real match situation. The strikers need encouragement and motivation in order to win the ball.

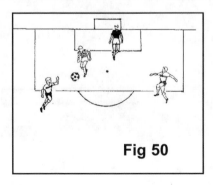

Fig 50

No.	Objectives	Age	Developing the Games	Common Problems
51	Paying attention. Concentration. Positioning.	17-18	A goalkeeper in goal with a 'fly' nearby (he later swaps roles with other players). 3-4 players with a number of balls on each wing. On the signal a player (with a ball) runs towards the goal. If the run is parallel to the goal line then the goalkeeper stands on the near post (not beyond it) so that there is no angle for the shot. But if the attacker approaches diagonally then the goalkeeper comes off his line in order to try to narrow the angle for the shot. In both cases the striker always tries a shot and the 'fly' always looks to score if the goalkeeper fails to hold on to the ball. If the goalkeeper claims the ball successfully he immediately throws it to a designated player.	The goalkeeper sometimes runs off his line even if the striker has no angle for the shot (in a game a pass inside would leave an open goal). If the striker approaches the goal 'head-on' the goalkeeper sometimes fails to run out in order to narrow the angle. The strikers dribble around the goalkeeper when in this game they are obliged to shoot.

Fig 51

No.	Objectives	Age	Developing the Games	Common Problems
52	The most important consideration, positioning. Simulating real match situations.	17-18	A goalkeeper in goal with a 'fly' nearby (he later swaps roles with other players). 3-4 players with a number of balls on each wing. A player from beyond the edge of the 18-yard box passes the ball to a player on the wing who runs parallel to the goal line. He has two options: 1.Shoot and see what happens, trying to take the goalkeeper by surprise. 2.Play a 'killer' pass to the player who started the move, allowing him to shoot from the edge of the 18-yard box. The goalkeeper's positioning is crucial. He should cover his near post (not go beyond it) and if the pass is played inside he should run off his line to narrow the angle. The goalkeeper has two attempts (one from each wing) and then swaps and has a rest.	Poor positioning (going beyond the near post or always waiting for the 'killer' pass). The player who shoots gets too close to the goal (the player who receives the pass should wait a moment while the goalkeeper re-positions). The goalkeeper forgets to throw the ball out after he claims it.

No.	Objectives	Age	Developing the Games	Common Problems
53	Paying attention. Concentration. Imagination. Reading the game. Long passing.	18-20	18 players, 9 balls and 3 goalkeepers. Pitch size is from the edge of one 18-yard box to the other. The outfield players play long passes to one another. The goalkeepers run all over the pitch trying to intercept the passes. The goalkeepers can intercept however they like (using body, feet, hands, jumping diving). When a ball is intercepted it is either thrown long to another player or the goalkeeper places it on the ground and runs with it a while before playing a long pass. The interception could involve control, run and pass without any use of hands.	The goalkeepers tend to stay in the same area, which rules out any chance of a surprise intervention. They should roam freely around the whole pitch. The goalkeepers pay little attention to passing (it is up to the coach to point out strengths and weaknesses, praise, encourage and motivate).

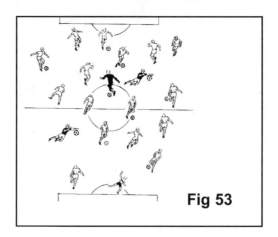

Fig 53

No.	Objectives	Age	Developing the Games	Common Problems
54	Developing the goalkeeper as a 'sweeper'. Playing the 'simple' game. Reading the game.	17-18	4 Goalkeepers. 1 plays in goal and the other 3 act as passive defenders playing flat somewhere between the 18-yard box and the halfway line. There are also various pairs that intervene as strikers. On the coach's signal 2 players advance down the right starting from the halfway line and run behind the defense. At the same time the goalkeeper runs off his line to cover the wide open space left behind the defenders. While this takes place the coach volleys a ball to the strikers. The goalkeeper has to resolve the situation as best he can. Sometimes the coach delivers the ball so that the goalkeeper has to head it clear. The same goalkeeper repeats the exercise trying to stop an attack from the left wing. All the goalkeepers swap roles.	Some goalkeepers try to dribble the ball. They should learn that it is always best to play safe under these circumstances (the goal is left unguarded) and so they should kick the ball into the stands. Many goals are scored because a poor clearance rebounds off an attacker. Kicking the ball out of play gives the goalkeeper and the defense time to reorganize.

Fig 54

No.	Objectives	Age	Developing the Games	Common Problems
55	Dealing with crosses. Heading. Running off the line. Catching. Releasing the ball quickly. Simulating real match situations.	17-18	A player on each wing with various balls each ready to make crosses. 3 attackers try to head a goal from the cross and a goalkeeper in goal. The goalkeeper tries to claim the ball although on occasion he can punch it clear. The strikers do their best to score just as they would during a proper match. Each time the goalkeeper claims the ball successfully he throws it to the next player who is going to cross the ball standing somewhere near the halfway line. This player controls the ball on the turn, runs to the by-line and centers the ball. The players swap and rotate on a regular basis.	Poor crosses. The goalkeeper does not time his run. Lack of bravery. Not jumping high enough. Forgetting to throw the ball out after it has been claimed.
56	Heading. Jumping. Simulating real match situations. Paying attention. Concentration. Positioning.	17-18	2 '5-a-side' heading games are played each on a pitch measuring 20 x 12 yards. Regulation size goals are used. The game involves tight marking. Free-kicks, throw-ins and corners are taken on the volley. When the goalkeeper claims the ball or has a goal-kick he puts it back into play with a jumping header. After 15-20 minutes the winning teams in each game face each other and the losing teams do the same.	The goalkeeper lets the play get very close to the goal. He should intervene even if it means using his fists. The goalkeepers forget to head the ball back in play. The goalkeepers do not organize their team. The goalkeeper is the boss!

Fig 55

Fig 58

No.	Objectives	Age	Developing the Games	Common Problems
57	Heading. Jumping. Simulating real match situations. Paying attention. Concentration. Positioning.	18-20	The same as the previous game but this time there are only 3 goals. The goalkeeper playing in the central goal is involved in both games at the same time. If he gets the ball there is no restriction on how he puts the ball back in play (the other 2 goalkeepers have to use a jumping header). If the ball goes out of play one of the defenders goes to get it as the goalkeeper in the center concentrates on the other game. The goalkeepers swap roles regularly as it is particularly tiring playing in the central goal.	Inability to concentrate on both games at once. Not shouting instructions to the team (the goalkeeper in the central goal has to organize the players in both games).
58	Balance. Coordination. Spatial orientation. Improvisation. Jumping.	17-18	A goalkeeper in goal holding a ball. The 'fly' nearby and various other players between the edge of the 6-yard box and the penalty spot. The goalkeeper bounces the ball as hard as he can and then jumps to catch it. The 'fly' does his best to head it. If the goalkeeper catches the ball he throws it out to the players waiting and does a forward roll before trying to save the header that is directed back towards the goal. The 'fly' is always ready to take advantage of any rebound. If the goalkeeper claims the ball he throws it out again and the exercise starts from the beginning. The players swap on a regular basis.	Occasionally a goalkeeper will feel light-headed as he jumps for the ball. The goalkeeper has a lot to think about and he cannot afford to make a mistake. This is a difficult task to achieve.

No.	Objectives	Age	Developing the Games	Common Problems
59	Ball control. Long passing. Dribbling. Simulating real match situations. This game is best played with a 'jet-ball' machine. The machine offers accuracy and consistency and therefore is better than using the 3 strikers.	17-18	3 goalkeepers. 1 plays in goal, 1 rests and 1 acts as the 'fly'. There are 3 other players 30 yards away each with various balls and well spread out. These 3 players take turns shooting at goal. The goalkeeper cannot use his hands or arms to save the ball. Once the goalkeeper has got the ball under control he kicks it back to the shooter. Of course, the goalkeeper has to deal with the nuisance caused by the 'fly' (who is outside the area when the shot is taken) as he tries to control and then pass the ball back. Each goalkeeper faces three shots before swapping.	Poor control gives the 'fly' a chance to score. The goalkeeper tries to dribble when it is best to simply pass as quickly as possible. If the goalkeeper dribbles he should do it from a safe distance not with the 'fly' close to the ball.
60	Saving volleys (good improvisation is needed). Releasing the ball quickly and intelligently.	17-18	Pitch size 18 x 12 yards. This is a game of '3 v 3'. 1 goalkeeper and 2 outfield players per team. There is also a 'neutral player on each wing. The ball is passed with the hand and shots are taken on the volley. The goalkeepers have to be very alert as shots can be taken at any time from anywhere. If the goalkeeper gets the ball he passes it to the player in the best position to receive it.	The goalkeepers lack concentration. They do not anticipate the shots. The coach needs to value and praise the goalkeepers when they produce good passes as this is a crucial skill.

Fig 59

Fig 62

No.	Objectives	Age	Developing the Games	Common Problems
61	Saving volleys (good improvisation is needed). Releasing the ball quickly and intelligently	18-20	The same as the previous game. Pitch size 18 x 12 yards. This is a game of '3 v 3'. 1 goalkeeper and 2 outfield players per team. There are no 'neutral players. Shots can be taken after passing the ball to yourself. This new element means that the goalkeeper has to concentrate even more as he has no idea when a shot will be taken.	The goalkeepers lack concentration. They do not anticipate the shots. The coach needs to value and praise the goalkeepers when they produce good passes as this is a crucial skill.
62	Positioning. Intuition. Anticipation. Diving. Releasing the ball quickly.	17-18	Various games played on pitches measuring 20 x 12 yards. There is a player at each corner and a goalkeeper in the middle who can move around(2 other goalkeepers wait their turn). The idea of the game is for players on one pitch to pass the ball to players on another without it being intercepted by the goalkeeper. Players on the same pitch are not allowed to pass to each other. A goalkeeper with good positioning sense does well in this game. If a goalkeeper gets the ball he throws a long pass to another goalkeeper on another pitch. Each time a goalkeeper makes a throw he earns a point. If goalkeepers forget to throw they do not earn the point.	Players around the same rectangle pass to each other. Poor positioning by the goalkeepers. Forgetting to throw the ball to a goalkeeper in the distance (some kick it).

No.	Objectives	Age	Developing the Games	Common Problems
63	Mobility. Anticipation. Getting a 'feel' for the game. Diving. Releasing the ball quickly.	17-18	3 goalkeepers willing to work very hard. A small-sized 'round' is formed where 5 players encircle a goalkeeper. The players play freely and dribble, use feints and dummies and pass with the intention of keeping possession. The goalkeeper tries to intercept the ball. He runs and dives in a bid to win the ball but if he is not successful he has to scramble back into position in the middle as quickly as possible. If he wins the ball he throws a long pass to the other 2 goalkeepers who are jogging in the distance. The goalkeepers swap regularly as this is a very tiring game. Each time the goalkeeper makes a throw he earns 1 point.	All the players play at a comfortable pace and the game lacks intensity. The players should be very active and mobile. The goalkeeper does not 'read' the game and therefore fails to anticipate well.

Fig 63

No.	Objectives	Age	Developing the Games	Common Problems
64	Multi-tasking. Concentration. Quick reflexes. Tactical awareness. General technical improvement. (The coach should explain clearly the benefits of this exercise to the goalkeepers. If they do not the goalkeepers might think this exercise is nonsensical. If a goal is scored when they are trying to save another ball they might become dejected and apathetic).	17-18	A goalkeeper stands in a goal positioned in the middle of the pitch. Other goalkeepers are close by (1 in either half of the pitch) and they take turns acting as the 'fly' until they swap and it is time to go in goal. A different game takes place in both halves of the pitch. There is a 'neutral' player in each game and he always plays with the team in possession to give the attack numerical superiority. Only the goalkeeper and the 2 players acting as the 'fly' are allowed in the center circle. The goalkeeper is involved in both games and so needs total concentration. If he gets possession of a ball he gives it straight to the 'fly' in that half of the pitch and concentrates on the other game. The goalkeepers swap on a regular basis.	Poor concentration as the goalkeepers are not used to doing so many different things at once. A goalkeeper is hit or concedes a goal because he did not even see the ball coming (this is not a good sign!). The strikers enter the center-circle. This is not allowed.

No.	Objectives	Age	Developing the Games	Common Problems
65	Paying attention. Concentration. Analyzing the game. Tactical awareness. General tactical improvement (both as a goalkeeper as a an outfield player).	17-18	Half the pitch. 3 goals. 1 in the middle and 1 on each wing. The game involves 6 goalkeepers and 17 outfield players. 3 goalkeepers play in the goal and the others play as outfield players until they swap roles. There are 10 balls on the pitch and the players try to claim one, beat any challenger and then score in one of the goals. A player who fails to claim a ball challenges for one so that he has the opportunity to dribble and shoot. The goalkeepers concentrate on all the balls in order to anticipate any threat on their goal. If they save a ball it is thrown to one of the coaches who puts it back in play.	Goalkeepers sometimes concede goals because they do not even see the ball coming. The goalkeepers make little effort when they play as outfield players (this is a mistake as this type of exercise is very useful for them). Some players shoot at a goal where the goalkeeper is already in the process of saving another shot (this player needs to go to another goal).
66	Paying attention. Concentration. Analyzing the game. Tactical awareness. General tactical improvement (both as a goalkeeper as a an outfield player).	17-18	Half the pitch. 3 goals. 1 in the middle and 1 on each wing. The game involves 6 goalkeepers and 17 outfield players. 3 goalkeepers play in the goal and the others play as outfield players until they swap roles. There are only 8 balls. Players do not have to dribble. But it is obligatory to play the 'one-two' with a teammate before shooting. For this reason 4 of the 20 players (the 3 goalkeepers not in goal and one other player) carry bibs and can only return the ball 'first-time' (acting as the wall for the 'one-two'). The goalkeepers swap on a regular basis.	Goalkeepers sometimes concede goals because they do not even see the ball coming. The goalkeepers make little effort when they play as outfield players (this is a mistake as this type of exercise is very useful for them). Some players shoot at a goal where the goalkeeper is already in the process of saving another shot (this player needs to go to another goal). Players shoot without playing the 'one-two'. Others play the 'one-two' but then fail to shoot.

No.	Objectives	Age	Developing the Games	Common Problems
67	Paying attention. Concentration. Analyzing the game. Anticipation. Improving technique as outfield players. Strength in the '1 v 1' confrontations.	18-20	Pitch size is half the pitch playing width-ways. '7 v 7' passing game maximum 'two-touch' playing the moves in 'the method'. There are no goals. A goal is scored when a player goes over the opposition's goal-line (what is usually the wing) with the ball. This means that the goalkeeper has to be very alert as he needs to 'read' the game and has to use his feet, so it helps if he can anticipate where any potential threat is coming from so that he can cut out the passes. He is involved in numerous '1 v 1' situations (in this case the goalkeeper can use his hands and the striker is not limited by the number of touches he can take).	Inability to 'read' the passes made by the opposition. Some goalkeepers use their hands when only feet are allowed. Ironically, they do not always use their hands in the '1 v1' situations. It takes time for the goalkeeper to realize that he acts as a 'sweeper' and so has to cover a lot of ground.

Fig 67

No.	Objectives	Age	Developing the Games	Common Problems
68	Knowledge of the system of play. Analyzing the game. The ability to 'read' the game quickly. Effective organization of teammates. Being assertive.	18-20	'11 v 11'. The coach speaks with the goalkeepers before the game and tells them to watch and analyze the game while constantly giving instructions to the rest of the team. The coach does not intervene during the game but makes a note of all the positive and negative points. The next day the goalkeepers have a theoretical session where the coach goes through each point with each one. Then the goalkeepers try to address any problems discussed during another '11 v 11' game.	Some goalkeepers are in a world of their own and do not communicate well with the rest of the team. Others are too shy to call out instructions. Some goalkeepers shout loudly and clearly but what they shout is of little use to anyone.
69	Lots of shots on goal so that the goalkeepers are kept busy. The ability to 'read' the game. Support teammates. Concentration.	18-20	A portable goal is positioned 20 yards away from a regulation size goal. 3 goalkeepers take turns doing the exercise. The game is '3 v 3' (2 outfield players and 2 goalkeepers). The players should be as evenly matched as possible. The basic idea of the game is to shoot as often as possible. Dribbling, the 'one-two' (also with the goalkeeper) and other moves in 'the method' are also performed. The players can shoot from anywhere. The goalkeepers are constantly saving shots.	The goalkeepers lack concentration. They do not come off their line to narrow the angle. Once the ball has been claimed the ball is not released quickly enough (the goalkeeper should always initiate the attacks)

Fig 69

No.	Objectives	Age	Developing the Games	Common Problems
70	Paying attention. Concentration. Quick reflexes. Controlling the space around you. Coordination. Releasing the ball quickly.	19-21	3 goalkeepers frequently swap roles. 1 plays in goal. 1 acts as the 'fly' and the other rests. 2 strikers shoot at the same time from a distance of 25 yards. The goalkeeper tries to stop both the balls from going into the net. If he is unable to catch the balls he uses his arms or legs to deflect or block the ball (not forgetting that the 'fly' waits to latch onto any rebound). If he holds onto the second ball, he throws it out to the goalkeeper resting. Once the strikers (who should all have a powerful shot) have shot twice the goalkeepers change roles. The goalkeeper who lets in least goals is the winner.	The goalkeepers find it hard to get used to the game at first. One striker shoots powerfully and the other produces a weak effort (this round of shots is void). If the strikers are too far away to produce an effective shot they can move closer.
71	Paying attention. Concentration. Quick reflexes. Controlling the space around you. Coordination.	19-21	The goalkeepers are in pairs and they stand 2-3 yards apart. The game is 'one-touch'. One goalkeeper throws a ball while the other kicks one. This is an awkward game because the players are so close together.	If the kicking and throwing technique is poor it is very difficult to play this game effectively. Those who have good technique and coordination play with ease and do very well.

Fig 70

No.	Objectives	Age	Developing the Games	Common Problems
72	Paying attention. Concentration. Quick reflexes. Catching. Volleys.	19-21	Two goals, 1 regulation goal and another positioned on the edge of the 18-yard box. Two players per team. A goalkeeper in each goal and a 'fly' near each of the goalkeepers. The goalkeepers (both at the same time) try to volley the ball into the goal opposite. The 'fly' tries to claim the ball and score only if the ball rebounds off the goalkeeper or the woodwork. If this happens the goalkeeper needs to react quickly in order to prevent the 'fly' from scoring a goal. The goalkeepers swap and rest after 3 volleys. The team (the goalkeeper and the 'fly') that scores the most goals wins.	All the players react slowly to rebounds. Sometimes the goalkeeper is unopposed as he claims the ball or the 'fly' scores without opposition. Some goalkeepers move too close to the other goal before shooting on the volley (the other goalkeeper can take advantage of this by playing a lob over his head)
73	Paying attention. Concentration. Quick reflexes. Focused and peripheral vision. Catching. Deflecting the ball. Volleys.	19-21	3 cones form a triangle 4 yards apart. These form 3 goals which are defended by only one goalkeeper at a time. 3 other goalkeepers (each with a ball in their hands) take turns trying to score in the goal opposite them. The goalkeeper positions himself as best he can (as he never knows who is going to shoot) so that he can see all the shooters. If he saves a volley he swaps with the player who took the shot. After 3-4 shots the goalkeeper swaps with one of the shooters. The number of goals scored and especially the number of shots saved are tallied at the end of the game.	Some goalkeepers do not take up a good position between the 3 shooters so that he monitors each one (this is difficult but some attempts are poor). The shooters always follow the same order which helps the goalkeeper tremendously.

No.	Objectives	Age	Developing the Games	Common Problems
74	Paying attention. Concentration. Quick reflexes. Mental agility. Coordination. Imagination.	19-25	4 goalkeepers take turns doing this exercise. Each player has a long rest after each intervention because the game is exhausting. 1 goalkeeper stands in goal and the coach stands on the edge of the 18-yard box with numerous balls. The coach calls out an instruction and the goalkeeper has to perform it in a special way. For example: if the coach shouts "right" then the goalkeeper has to dive to his left to save an imaginary ball. If the shout is "left" then he dives to his right. If the coach shouts "back" the goalkeeper moves forward and vice versa. If the shout is "jump" the goalkeeper sits and if "sit" he jumps. If the coach shouts "shot" and a direction then he shoots to the other side of the goal. The goalkeeper has to react and move as quickly as possible and take up the original 'starting' position after each movement.	Sometimes the goalkeepers do not react at all and remain stationary. This is due to the fact that they have to think of various things at once. The goalkeepers often follow the exact instructions given by the coach. The coach also makes mistakes. Perhaps shouting, "left" and shooting to the left side of the goal.

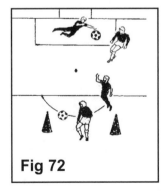

Fig 72

Fig 74

No.	Objectives	Age	Developing the Games	Common Problems
75	Paying attention Concentration. Quick reflexes. Catching. Deflecting the ball. Diving.	19-25	The coach stands on the edge of the 18-yard box opposite the goal with the 'jet-ball' machine. A goalkeeper is in goal with the 'fly' ready to latch on to any rebounds. 2 other goalkeepers awaiting their turn stand on the wings ready to receive the throw from the goalkeeper when he saves a shot. On the signal the goalkeeper runs from post to post while concentrating on the 'jet-ball' machine. The coach watches the goalkeeper and releases a ball when appropriate. The further away the machine the harder the shot. The ball is not shot as hard if it is released when the goalkeeper is running in the opposite direction.	Not concentrating on the ball heading towards the goal. Trying to hold on to the ball instead of parrying or deflecting it for a corner (not towards the 'fly'). The coach needs to make sure that he uses a wide range of shots unless he wants to concentrate on a particular weak aspect of the goalkeeper's game.

No.	Objectives	Age	Developing the Games	Common Problems
76	Paying atten-tion. Concentration. Focused and peripheral vision. Jumping. Improving punching technique. Using feet.	19-21	4 goalkeepers involved in this game. 3 (each hold-ing a ball) form a circle while the other player is in the middle about 6-8 yards away bouncing up and down on a mini-tram-poline. At any given moment, 1 of the players throws up a high ball for the goalkeeper on the mini-trampoline to jump and punch away. Then another player throws a ball up and so on until the coach decides to swap the players around. The goalkeeper on the mini-trampoline has no idea which of the 3 players is going to throw the ball up and so he has to twist and turn as he bounces in order to keep an eye on all the balls. Each goal-keeper makes a note of all effective punches as indicated by the coach.	Not concentrating on all 3 balls. Not timing the bounce and jump in order to punch the ball cleanly. Not fully extending the arm at the moment the ball is struck.

No.	Objectives	Age	Developing the Games	Common Problems
77	Paying attention. Concentration. Quick reflexes. Overcoming difficulties. Analyzing distribution. Quick decision making. Positioning. Choosing the best pass to make. From now on the goalkeeper does not only have to distribute the ball quickly but he has various options and has to choose the best. This is such an important aspect of goalkeeping that it should be repeated frequently.	19-21	4 goalkeepers who frequently swap roles: 2 ready to receive a pass, 1 as the 'fly' and the other plays in goal. 3 strikers take turns shooting from the edge of the 18-yard box. The 'fly' is more of a nuisance during this game as he stands sideways-on in front of the goalkeeper to obscure his line of vision. He tries not to get hit by the ball but if he can re-direct a shot he will. The goalkeeper knows which striker is about to shoot but has to overcome the difficulty posed by the 'fly'. If the goalkeeper gets the ball he can either play the pass short or long out towards the halfway line. He needs to choose the best pass to make as the longer option is not always the best. (In a game a marked player can lose his marker and run into space. If the goalkeeper 'reads' this possibility and anticipates it then he plays the ball into the space for his teammate to take in his stride).	The goalkeeper is 'put off' by the 'fly' and he either laughs or becomes irritated. Either way, he loses concentration. Some players who act as the 'fly' do not dare inconvenience the goalkeeper too much whereas they should do everything in their power to make his job difficult. The goalkeepers find it difficult to decide on the appropriate pass to make.

Fig 77

No.	Objectives	Age	Developing the Games	Common Problems
78	Paying attention. Concentration. Quick reflexes. Reading the game. Quick decision making. Positioning. Choosing the best pass to make.	20-21	A goalkeeper in goal. There is no 'fly' in this game. 3 defenders and 3 strikers simultaneously play '1 v 1' on the edge of the 18-yard box. The goalkeeper monitors the progress of each duel and anticipates where the ball is likely to come from. Perhaps if a ball is not released after a reasonable length of time then he chooses the best time to dive in amongst the two players to claim the ball and then pass it to one of the other goalkeepers waiting. Next he immediately gets back in position concentrating on the other pairings. When a player breaks free and heads towards goal the goalkeeper stands tall and holds his ground, trying to prevent a goal. The goalkeepers swap after they have tried to save 3 balls because this is a very physically demanding game.	The goalkeepers do not anticipate well which striker is about to get past his opponent. They forget to immediately concentrate on the other '1 v 1' confrontations in progress after they make an intervention. Some become demoralized as a goal is scored as they were concentrating on another ball. Point out that they are not 'Superman' and so this is inevitable.

Fig 78

No.	Objectives	Age	Developing the Games	Common Problems
79	Paying attention. Concentration. Quick reflexes. Reading the game. Positioning. Choosing the best pass to make.	19-20	This is a similar game to the previous one but this time there are only 2 defenders against 3 attackers. The latter approach at the same time, each running with a ball. They try to take advantage of the numerical superiority in order to get a clear chance on goal. Obviously, one of the strikers is unmarked and so usually gets to threaten the goal. The goalkeeper has to watch and anticipate which player is likely to cause the danger. Whether he saves the ball or a goal is scored he has to immediately concentrate on the other pairings. The goalkeeper passes the ball out each time he claims a ball. The goalkeeper swaps with another once he has dealt with all 3 balls.	Forgetting to immediately concentrate on the other ball or balls once they have made an intervention. The attacks happen so quickly that the goalkeeper is often out of position. Not choosing the best pass when distributing the ball.

Fig 79

No.	Objectives	Age	Developing the Games	Common Problems
80	Paying attention. Concentration. Positioning. Overcoming difficulties. Choosing the best pass to make.	19-21	4 goalkeepers take turns doing this exercise. 2 attackers ready to shoot. 1 is in the midfield and the other 20 yards from goal. The player in the midfield area runs towards goal and when he is about 30 yards away he releases a powerful shot. The job of the other attacker is to run into the area and try to dribble round the goalkeeper. There is also a 'fly' ready to impede the goalkeeper and score from any rebound. The goalkeeper changes his position depending on the situation. When faced by the shot from distance he needs to stand a few inches off his line because the ball is in the air a long time and it could reach him as it is on its way down. If the goalkeeper is too far off his line the ball could fly over his head and into the goal. When confronted by the player in the area the goalkeeper needs to sprint off his line in order to narrow the angle. The 'fly' gets in the goalkeeper's way as he runs out (this simulates what some defenders do involuntarily). The other 2 goalkeepers jog some distance from the action ready play when the coach gives the signal.	Some goalkeepers still take up poor positions. They come too far off their line for long shots and stay back when faced by the player in the area. When this happens, psychologically they are already beaten whereas if the goalkeeper positions himself correctly all the onus is on the attacker.

No.	Objectives	Age	Developing the Games	Common Problems
81	Positioning. Technique using hands and feet. Long passes. Simulating real match situations.	19-21	4 goalkeepers. 1 in goal. 1 as the 'fly' waiting outside the area and 2 waiting their turn near the halfway line. The coach is in the center circle with 5 balls. He shoots on the volley so that the ball lands roughly near the penalty spot. The goalkeeper has to control the ball without using his hands (on thigh, chest or with feet) and run with the ball in the area until the 'fly' approaches. The goalkeeper then picks up the ball and throws it out to one of the goalkeepers waiting near the halfway line. As he throws the ball out, the coach volleys another ball into the area. The goalkeeper judges the flight of the ball and moves to catch it. Then, with the 'fly' getting in his way, he kicks the ball out on the volley to the other goalkeeper waiting near the halfway line. The goalkeepers swap roles regularly. The coach is particularly interested in how the goalkeepers claim the ball, how they attack and how they defend.	Some goalkeepers have poor ball control which means the 'fly' has time to cause more of a nuisance (playing well as an outfield player can only be improved with practice). Sometimes the 'fly' is in the area for the first volley from the coach (he needs to be outside to give the goalkeeper some space to try to control the ball). The long throws and passes to the halfway line are poor.

Fig 82

Fig 83

No.	Objectives	Age	Developing the Games	Common Problems
82	Passing with a throw. Concentration. Quick reflexes. Overcoming difficulties. Goalkeeper and outfield player technique.	19-21	Pitch size 20 yards. Regulation size goals. 4 goalkeepers playing in pairs. They take turns playing in goal or as the 'fly'. 1 goalkeeper is carrying the ball when he suddenly throws it towards the other goal. The other goalkeeper tries to save it but the 'fly' does his best to obstruct him, get the ball himself and score or shoot from any rebound. Sometimes the goalkeeper passes directly to the 'fly' instead of throwing directly at goal. This is part of the game and the defending goalkeeper has to deal with it. After 3 throws the goalkeepers swap roles. The pair who score the most goals wins.	Sometimes the 'fly' is tempted to use his hands. This is not allowed as he should play as an outfield player. Some goalkeepers get annoyed with the 'fly'. The coach needs to point out that the work performed by the 'fly' forms the basis of the exercise.
83	Shots on goal. Concentration. Quick reflexes. Overcoming difficulties.	19-21	The same as above but this time the pitch size is 30 yards with a line marking the halfway line. The goalkeeper runs with the ball until he gets close to the halfway line and shoots at goal. The other goalkeeper tries to save the ball while being impeded by the 'fly'. Then this goalkeeper takes a turn at shooting. The pairing who scores the most goals wins.	The 'fly' drops back to receive a pass from his teammate. This is not allowed as he needs to stand fairly close to the goal. Sometimes the 'fly' makes little effort to impede the goalkeeper.

No.	Objectives	Age	Developing the Games	Common Problems
84	Paying atten-tion. Concentration. Reading the game. Anticipation. Diving for-wards. Releasing the ball quickly. Choosing the best pass to make.	19-25	3 goalkeepers, 1 plays in goal and 2 wait their turn near the halfway line. 9 outfield players are split into groups of 3 with a ball per trio. They pass the ball to each other near the halfway line. There are 2 portable walls positioned in line with each post just beyond the 18-yard box. On the signal the first trio of attackers head directly for goal with the middle player in possession of the ball. The other 2 play-ers run round the walls waiting to receive the ball. The player on the ball feints and dummies but eventually shoots against one of the walls so that the rebound is perfect for the player on the other side to run on to. The goalkeeper has to 'read' the intentions of the play-er passing the ball and if possible run out and dive to claim the ball before a shot is taken. If this is not possible then he runs out to narrow the angle. If the goalkeeper claims the ball he immediately throws it out to one of the other goalkeepers. After 3 inter-ventions the goalkeepers swap.	The attacker does not disguise his pass. The player who receives the pass does not shoot but passes it to the play-er on the other side. This is not allowed as it leaves the goalkeeper powerless to stop a goal being scored. The player who does not receive the pass stops running when he should continue in case there is a rebound and he has the opportunity to score. The goalkeeper does not 'read' the move.

Fig 85

No.	Objectives	Age	Developing the Games	Common Problems
85	Paying attention. Concentration. Reading the game. Anticipation. Positioning. Diving forwards. Releasing the ball quickly. Choosing the best pass to make.	19-25	3 goalkeepers, 1 plays in goal and 2 wait near the halfway line. 6 outfield players do the following: 2 are defenders positioned on the edge of the 18-yard box 10 yards apart. They are ready to intervene on an individual basis. 2 are attackers who are positioned fairly near to the defenders but closer to the wings. The other 2 players have a ball each and are in the midfield area of the pitch. They are also 10 yards apart. 1 of these players runs with the ball towards the defender opposite. There are two possible moves: play the 'one-two' with the attacker or try to dribble round the defender. The goalkeeper is ready to deal with either situation. If the 'one-two' is played the goalkeeper anticipates the move and runs off his line, acting like a 'sweeper' ready to dive to claim the ball if necessary. If the attacker dribbles into the box then the goalkeeper runs out to narrow the angle. If the goalkeeper gets the ball he immediately throws it out to one of the goalkeepers near the halfway line. After the move has ended the second attacker runs forward and the same scenario takes place down the other flank. The goalkeepers swap roles after facing two attacks or shots. All the other players swap frequently to experience each role.	Some goalkeepers do not react when they see the attacker heading towards the goal. Others react late and do not challenge for the ball for fear of getting injured. The throws are executed immediately but they are not always directed to the goalkeeper in the best position to receive the ball.

No.	Objectives	Age	Developing the Games	Common Problems
86	Paying attention. Concentration. Quick reflexes. Jumping. Diving. Explosive power. Volleys.	19-21	Pitch size 4 x 6 yards divided by a net 4 ft high. There is a goalkeeper on each side, positioned centrally just beyond the playing area. The game starts when one of the players volleys the balls over the net. The other player desperately tries to get to the ball in order to head it before it bounces in the court. If successful, he volleys it back over the net. If the player manages to head the ball back over the net then the exercise turns into a heading game until one of the players wins the round. If the ball bounces in the opposition's side of the court 3 points are awarded. If a header is made (it does not matter where the ball is directed) 1 point is awarded. The player who wins the heading round is awarded 2 points.	The volley is poorly directed and does not get to the other side of the court. If this happens the other player gets the ball and has a volley. The players do not dive for the ball If they did perhaps they could have headed it over to the other side of the net. Taking the volley from inside the court area is not allowed. If this happens the ball is handed to the other player.

Fig 86

Fig 87

Fig 88

No.	Objectives	Age	Developing the Games	Common Problems
87	Paying great attention. Multiple Concentration. Extraordinary improvisation. Reading the game. Multiple technical skills. Focused and peripheral vision. Will-power. Determination. Decision making capacity (quickly and correctly).	19-25	Pitch size 20 x 12 yards. Two heading games take place at the same time. 3-4 goalkeepers alternate with only one in goal at any one time. There are 12 players, 3 players in each team with similar heading ability (on an individual and collective basis). The goalkeeper concentrates on both balls which he can claim and then release as he wishes. He never goes to collect a ball if it goes out as he needs to concentrate on the other ball. This is a very tiring game for the goalkeepers (physically and mentally) and so they swap on a regular basis.	Some goalkeepers take a long time to get used to the game. Very few manage to control what happens in both games. Some take too long to make decisions. Some make rash decisions that are not always the most appropriate.
88	Quick reflexes. Concentration. Balance. Anticipation. Agility. Jumping. Catching. Passing with a throw. Long passes (feet)	19-21	2 goalkeepers in goal (as evenly matched as possible). 2 more goalkeepers with various balls each are 40 yards away, 1 on each wing. On the signal one of the goalkeepers plays a long and high pass into the area. The goalkeepers immediately do a forward roll, get up as quickly as possible and try to claim the ball. The successful player throws the ball out to the goalkeeper on the other wing. Then this player passes the ball into the box and the process is similar. The goalkeepers swap roles frequently.	Occasionally a goalkeeper forgets to do the forward roll. Some goalkeepers do not stand their ground when challenging for the ball. The passes are not always lofted enough (the goalkeepers defending the goal should have the opportunity to jump and dive to claim the ball).

No.	Objectives	Age	Developing the Games	Common Problems
89	Quick reflexes. Concentration. Balance. Agility. The technique of the outfield players.	19-25	2 goalkeepers in goal (as evenly matched as possible). 2 more goalkeepers with various balls each are 40 yards away, 1 on each wing. All the goalkeepers play as outfield players. One of the players on the wing kicks the ball into the box. The two goalkeepers do a forward roll and try to claim the ball by kicking it clear, heading it, using feet or body. The ideal option is to get the ball under control and pass it but this is not always possible. The game continues in this way and the goalkeepers swap frequently. Getting to the ball first earns 1 point. If the ball is controlled and a good pass is made 3 points are awarded.	Some coaches put players together who have similar goalkeeping ability. This is of no use here as the players need to be matched according to how good they are with their feet. They rarely try to get 3 points. In a game it is always best to play safe but this exercise is all about trying things and taking risks.

No.	Objectives	Age	Developing the Games	Common Problems
90	Concentration. Balance. Agility. Jumping. Catching. Releasing the ball quickly.	19-25	4 goalkeepers. 1 plays in goal, 1 acts as the 'fly' and the other 2 wait to receive a pass. The coach stands on the edge of the 18-yard box holding a ball with more at his feet. He throws the ball up high towards the goal and the goalkeeper jumps to catch it and throw it out to one of the other goalkeepers waiting on the wings. The goalkeeper immediately does a forward roll as the coach launches another ball towards the goal. As he gets up he locates the ball and tries to dive to claim it before it bounces. However, the 'fly' makes this awkward by getting in his way. If the ball bounces the goalkeeper dives to claim it anyway. Once he has the ball he throws it out to one of the wings. After every two interventions the goal-keepers swap roles.	Some goalkeepers stop when the 'fly' gets in their way. They have to keep going and find a way round him. Some goalkeepers are unable to cope because of the quick-thinking and the diverse coordination and movements involved. It is unusual for the 'fly' to perform his role prop-erly (he either does not get in the way or he is not bothered).

Fig 90

No.	Objectives	Age	Developing the Games	Common Problems
91	Agility. Coordination. Explosive power. Diving at feet. Releasing the ball quickly. Dribbling.	19-25	4 goalkeepers play a 'round' in a reduced playing area. They are positioned as follows: 2 are a long way from the 'round' ready to receive the long throw. 1 in the middle with the other player as an attacker together with the 5 outfield players that form the 'round'. Each attacker has to try to dribble round the goalkeeper in the middle before passing the ball to another player. The goalkeeper needs to anticipate the move and dive at the attacker's feet in order to claim the ball. If he gets the ball then he immediately throws it to one of the goalkeepers near the halfway line. Another ball is used and the game continues. The goalkeepers swap roles regularly as this is a very tiring exercise. The attackers also get tired so they take turns dribbling.	Some goalkeepers are a bit reluctant to dive at the attacker's feet. Sometimes the dive is too obvious and too early so the attacker has time to improvise and keep possession (the goalkeeper should dive across the player in the direction the ball is going). The goalkeeper goes from playing in the middle and immediately tries to dribble around the goalkeeper. He needs to wait until he is fully rested.

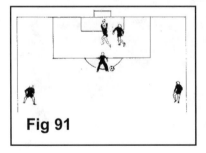

Fig 91

No.	Objectives	Age	Developing the Games	Common Problems
92	Paying attention. Concentration. Focused and peripheral vision. Dominating the space around you. Quick reflexes. Deflections. Catching. Stretching and diving. Releasing the ball quickly to the best-positioned teammate.	19-21	A 'round' played in an area 30 x 30 yards. 6 players form the circle. A goalkeeper is in the middle defending a goal. 2 more goalkeepers (one on each wing) jog waiting to receive the throw. There is a game of '3 v 3' taking place in the middle where the players can score from either side of the goal. The 6 players forming the circle always help the team in possession of the ball. The game is 'two-touch' and the players can only score with a header or volley, which cannot be executed immediately after the ball bounces. If the strike goes wide or if it is saved the game continues. If the goalkeeper catches the ball he immediately throws it out to the goalkeeper in the best position to receive it. This player returns the ball and the game continues. After a certain time the two teams swap roles with the players forming the circle. The goalkeepers swap roles frequently.	Shots are taken as soon as possession is won. The ball should be played to a player in the circle to begin the attack. Not using the 'neutral' players. Goals and the final pass are valued in this game. No passes are made over the goalkeeper's head to facilitate the strike from the other side of the goal. Lots of passing and few strikes on goal. The reverse is the ideal in this game.

No.	Objectives	Age	Developing the Games	Common Problems
93	Paying attention. Concentration. Quick reflexes. Deflecting. Catching. Stretching and diving. Releasing the ball quickly to the best-positioned teammate	19-25	Pitch size 30 x 15 yards. 4 goalkeepers. 1 in each goal and 2 more not on the pitch waiting their turn. The game involves 3 teams (teams A, B and C) of 3 players. The ball is carried and shots can only be taken as volleys, half-volleys or drop kicks. Team A attacks team B as team C rests. Later team B attacks team C and team A rests etc. A player can only shoot after receiving a high ball from a teammate or passing to himself (or feinting to make this move before passing to an unmarked teammate). The goalkeepers need to stay alert as these shots are never very easy to save. If the goalkeeper claims the ball he immediately passes it to one of the goalkeepers jogging on the wing. This goalkeeper immediately passes the ball to the team resting. The goalkeepers swap on a regular basis.	Too much passing. The idea of the game is to shoot. Shots are only taken near the goal. Shots can be taken from anywhere. Players do not play feints and dummies or pass to themselves.

Fig 93

Fig 94

No.	Objectives	Age	Developing the Games	Common Problems
94	Explosive power. Bravery. Concentration. Catching. Deflecting. Stretching and diving. Releasing the ball quickly.	19-25	A goalkeeper is surrounded by 4 players (one of these is a goalkeeper) 4 yards away. 2 goalkeepers jog on the wings waiting to receive a pass. The attackers shoot at an imaginary goal near the goalkeeper. He dives to his left or right to gather the ball or at least deflect it wide of the goal. If he claims a ball he immediately throws it out to one of the goalkeepers jogging on the wing. He then returns to face the rapid and incessant shots. The attackers should take advantage of any rebound. The goalkeepers swap frequently.	Some goalkeepers avoid trying to stop powerfully struck shots. This is not a good sign. Some shots go so wide of the goalkeeper that he has no chance to get near the ball. Some of the attackers get hit by the ball if they are not concentrating.
95	Playing in goal. Playing as an outfield player. Most important - the ability to 'read' the game. Making tactical decisions and helping teammates with positioning.	19-25	1 goalkeeper in goal. 4 defenders play zonal marking faced by 6 attackers. The goalkeeper has to play well in goal and organize and position his defense. If the goalkeeper gets the ball he passes it to one of the defenders and the defense tries to keep possession for 30 seconds (the goalkeeper also plays as an outfield player during this period). Once the time is up or possession is lost another 6 attackers head towards goal.	Some goalkeepers seem deaf and dumb whereas others continually shout instructions but have no idea what they are talking about. When the defenders get the ball some goalkeepers do not help out (conscious of their limitations as outfield players) but this is a wonderful opportunity to improve their ability as 'complete' players.

No.	Objectives	Age	Developing the Games	Common Problems
96	Simulating real match situations. Catching. Punching. Anticipation. Reading the game. Releasing the ball quickly. Coordinating positioning of teammates. Playing as a defender.	19-21	1 goalkeeper in goal and a player at each corner with various balls ready to make crosses into the box. The crosses are aimed at the penalty spot where 3 defenders (these are the goalkeepers who later swap roles) and 2 attackers are waiting to meet the ball. There are 2 more attackers waiting on the edge of the 18-yard box, ready to take advantage of any wayward crosses, deflections or poor clearances. The goalkeeper has to decide whether to come off his line to attempt to claim the cross. He also organizes the defenders. If he gets the ball he passes it to the player in the corner who did not make the cross. He runs with the ball to the midfield area, turns and heads to the by-line before crossing the ball into the box. The goalkeepers swap frequently and the attackers also take turns playing the 3 roles.	The goalkeeper does not shout for the ball as he runs and jumps to claim it. This causes misunderstandings and collisions with his defenders. This is why it is a good opportunity for the goalkeepers to act as defenders so that they see things from their perspective. Some defenders and attackers do not make enough effort. All the players need to treat the exercise as a real match.
97	Positioning. Concentration. Anticipation. The goalkeeper goes from defender to out-and-out attacker.	19-21	Pitch size 30 x 30 yards. 2 goals side by side at each end marked with cones. This is a game of '5 v 5'. All the players including the goalkeepers have to attack 2 goals. Apart from getting the goalkeepers to turn defense into attack the idea is for all the players to expand and improve their game.	Some goalkeepers can neither position themselves effectively nor help teammates with their positioning. Once they have the ball they are too slow at getting to the final third of the pitch.

No.	Objectives	Age	Developing the Games	Common Problems
98	Acting as a 'modern' goal-keeper (playing in goal and beyond the 18-yard box). Dual responsibility: Goalkeeper and 'sweeper'. The outfield players try to overcome the 'off-side' trap.	19-21	Pitch size 50 x 50 yards. This is a game of '4 v 4'. There is a line drawn across the whole width of the pitch 20 yards from each goal. The outfield players play in and shoot from the 10 yards in between these two areas. A player can only run into the 20 yard zone after a through ball has been played by a teammate. If he runs into this zone before the pass is made he is 'off-side'. The goal-keeper has to do his best to stop the runner from scoring. At first the player has to shoot before entering the 20 yard zone, but later, when the coach gives the signal, the players can try to dribble round the goalkeeper.	The goalkeepers are sometimes too far off their line and they are caught out by a long shot. Sometimes they do not 'read' the game well and so are slow to run off their line to challenge the player on the ball and narrow the angle. The defenders play in the 20 yard zone. This is not allowed, only the goalkeeper can defend this area.

Fig 98

No.	Objectives	Age	Developing the Games	Common Problems
99	Acting as a 'modern' goal-keeper (saving shots and preventing them from materializing). Dual responsibility: Save shots and anticipation narrowing the angle, bravery, ability to compete physically and releasing the ball quickly...)	19-22	Pitch size 50 x 50 yards. This is a game of '4 v 4'. There is a line drawn across the whole width of the pitch 20 yards from each goal. One player in each team is allowed to play close to the opposition's goal in a clear 'off-side' position. The rest of the players try to play with variety and imagination instead of just passing to this forward player all the time. They pass to each other, dribble and shoot. The goalkeeper has to cope with the long shots and the presence of the 'fly' (he is quicker and a lot more active and astute than in previous games). The goalkeeper tries to avoid goals being scored and once he claims the ball he plays a long pass to the 'fly' near the goal opposite or to another teammate in space. 3-4 goalkeepers swap roles regularly as this is a very tiring game. All the outfield players take turns playing as the 'fly'.	Lack of concentration means that the goal-keeper does not get to the ball in time. The 'fly' plays deep to receive the pass from his teammates. This is not allowed as he needs to always make space in and around the goalmouth area. The goalkeeper always passes to the 'fly' even when he is not in a good position to receive the ball and other team-mates are in space.
100	Acting as a 'modern' goal-keeper (playing in goal and beyond the 18-yard box). Dual responsibility: Goalkeeper and 'sweeper'. All players learn to deal with the 'off-side' trap.	19-22	Pitch size half the pitch played width-ways (with the goals on what are normally the wings). There are 4 goals at each end, one near each corner. This is a game of '7 v 7'. The teams play 'off-side' and so the defense pushes up as a unit. The goal-keeper has to defend both the goals and anticipate any long balls that get beyond the defenders.	Sometimes the goal-keepers do not 'read' the game well and so are slow to run off their line to intercept long balls or challenge the player on the ball and narrow the angle. Sometimes the goal-keeper times his run well but lacks the necessary ball skills with his feet to resolve the situation effectively.

No.	Objectives	Age	Developing the Games	Common Problems
101	Organize the defense. 'The players at the back control the players in front of them'(so the goalkeeper is the 'boss'). Analyzing the play. Concentration.	19-21	A portable goal is placed 18 yards from the halfway line. This is a game of '9 v 11'. The goalkeeper defends the goal and has 4 defenders near the middle of the pitch, 2 midfield players and 2 wingers in his team. The other team has 11 players. The team with 9 play the 'pressing' game, cover for each other and interchange positions and try to mount swift counter-attacks. The goalkeeper should organize his teammates.	Some goalkeepers have poor tactical awareness and so offer little help to the rest of the team. Lack of organization in the team with 9 players, without it the team has no chance of winning.

Fig 99

Fig 100

No.	Objectives	Age	Developing the Games	Common Problems
102	Paying attention. Concentration. The 'logic' of the game. Analyzing the play. Tactical improvisation.	19-21	This can be played as a '7v7', '9v9' or '11v11' where the pitch size changes according to the number of players. All the players practice the movements in 'the method' and the goalkeeper organizes and coordinates the defense. During the game the coach will give the signal for one of the players to move out of position (could be a defender or an attacker). He only gets back into position if the goalkeeper tells him where to move. This happens throughout the game. If the goalkeeper does not notice then the coach points out his mistake. If he quickly spots the poor positioning and shouts to his teammate to move back then the coach praises him.	Some players are brilliant at reading the game whereas others have little idea. Some even get a player to move who is in the correct position. Coaches should appreciate it when they have a goalkeeper with good tactical awareness and the ability to 'read' the game.

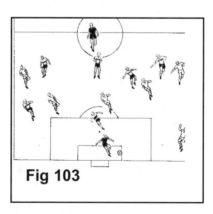

Fig 103

No.	Objectives	Age	Developing the Games	Common Problems
103	Playing as both defender and attacker. The ability to quickly turn defense into attack and vice versa. Goalkeepers should not only be able to play in goal but also start attacking moves. Technical skills of the outfield player (control, dribbling, feints and dummies passing etc).	19-21	Pitch size is half the pitch. Two teams of 6 players per team. 1 goalkeeper is in goal and the other goalkeeper plays near the halfway line (there is no goalmouth) and helps start the attacking move. The defending team plays as a unit adopting the zonal marking system in order to try to win back the ball. If the team wins possession they try to keep it by playing back and sideways passes (the goalkeeper should be the central player getting involved as much as possible). If the other team wins the ball back then (with the help of their goalkeeper) they start the attacking build-up again. After a while the teams swap sides and roles.	The goalkeepers with good 'soccer' skills look for the ball and enjoy the game. Those who have less ability tend to participate less. These are the players the game benefits most. Some goalkeepers lose the ball because they do not keep the game 'simple'
104	Analyzing the play. Assimilating the role of 'sweeper'. Assimilating the role of attacker. Technique of the outfield players. Using this valuable experience when playing in goal.	19-25	Pitch size regulation size. This is a game of '11 v 11'. 2 goalkeepers play as 'sweepers'. The idea is to help them understand, 'read' the game and anticipate the play as outfield players. During the second half they swap and play as out and out attackers. This helps them appreciate the problems faced by the forward players and when they play in goal they should be able to 'read' the game and anticipate what is likely to happen. This exercise should be repeated from time to time but not on a repeated basis.	When playing in attack the goalkeepers are very selfish. This needs to be addressed. They do not always take the exercise seriously when playing as 'sweepers'. They should always play in the designated positions but some roam around the pitch and do not stick to this specific task.

No.	Objectives	Age	Developing the Games	Common Problems
105	Multi-tasking. Concentration. Extraordinary improvisation. Mental and physical agility. Focused and peripheral vision. Intervention quality and quantity.	19-25	Pitch size is half the pitch. Two games of 4 outfield players in each team take place at the same time. The game is maximum 'three-touch', man-to-man marking and involves playing the moves in 'the method and the 'off-side' trap. There is a goalkeeper in each goal who has to concentrate on both the balls on the pitch. They ignore the ball if it goes wide and totally focus on the other one in play. If they catch one of the balls they immediately throw it back in play. This is such a tiring game that it is a good idea to have 3-4 goalkeepers taking turns playing in short bursts.	Lack of concentration means that the goalkeeper concedes lots of goals. All goalkeepers take a while to adapt to all the things they have to concentrate on at the same time but gradually they all improve mentally, physically, tactically and technically.

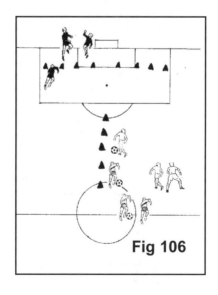

Fig 106

No.	Objectives	Age	Developing the Games	Common Problems
106	Paying attention. Concentration. Positioning. Quick reflexes. Explosive power. Acceleration. (By this stage the goalkeepers should be comfortable diving to either side but this is not always the case. If this occurs it is a good idea to ask the goalkeeper to stand slightly to one side of the goal so that he has to dive to his weaker side more often).	22-32	1 goalkeeper in the regulation size goal. There is a line of 4 cones 2 yards apart, starting in line with the post and stretching to the right parallel to the byline. Another line of cones stretches to the left starting opposite the left post. 5 yards beyond the penalty spot and stretching towards the halfway line there is another line of 5 cones each 2 yards apart. There are 3 players with a ball each positioned at the first and the last cone. On the signal a player from each group runs round the cones in an attempt to be the first to shoot. The goalkeeper sets off at the same time and runs in and out of the cones to his right and tries to get in position to save the shots. However, the goalkeeper has an extra problem: there is a goalkeeper at cone number 2 and 4 who does his best to hold and generally impede the progress of the runner. They are not allowed to use their feet and the runner is supposed to 'fight back' and struggle to 'break free'. Once the shots have been taken, 2 more players set off and the goalkeeper runs to his left where he faces 2 more goalkeepers positioned at cones 2 and 4. After these two attempts the goalkeeper swaps with one of the players doing the hassling.	The key to this game is good positioning. But the goalkeeper is usually tired or disorientated after the sprint and struggles around the cones. The goalkeepers take too long to get beyond the obstacles and so do not get back to the goal in time. Sometimes the second shot is not taken (ideally, this should be taken immediately after the first one). Lack of concentration and quick reflexes.

No.	Objectives	Age	Developing the Games	Common Problems
107	Paying attention. Concentration. Positioning. Quick reflexes. Running with the ball. Dribbling. Explosive power.	22-32	This is a very similar game to the previous one except this time the goalkeeper is not impeded by other goalkeepers. However, he has to run around the cones and back again and once he has gone past the last one he positions himself ready to save the shots.	Poor positioning. Lack of concentration. Poor reflexes. Difficulty saving the second shot.
108	Paying attention. Concentration. Quick reflexes. Coordination. Stretching and diving. Deflecting. Catching. Explosive power.	22-32	1 goalkeeper in goal and 2 'flies' nearby. The jet-ball machine is positioned 20 yards from the goal. There are 3 cones 1 yard apart on the goal-line. The goalkeeper runs in and out of the cones and waits to dive to save the powerfully placed shot from the jet-ball machine. The other 2 players are ready to take advantage of any rebound and so the goalkeeper has to be prepared to try to save a second time of necessary. The goalkeepers swap after they have faced 2 shots. A note is taken of the number of goals conceded.	Lack of concentration. Poor reflexes. Not reacting to the rebounds.

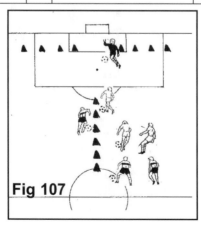

Fig 107

No.	Objectives	Age	Developing the Games	Common Problems
109	Multi-tasking. Concentration. Quick reflexes. Positioning. Coordination. Stretching and diving. Deflecting. Catching. Explosive power.	22-32	The coach is in the 18-yard box with a ball and he moves around observing the positioning of the goalkeeper. The goalkeeper is also aware that the jet-ball is situated 30 yards from goal and could release a powerful shot at any time. The coach shoots at goal if the goalkeeper is poorly positioned. Then the machine shoots and the coach continues to move about to see if the goalkeeper takes up the correct position until the jet-ball releases another powerful shot. After 2 shots the goalkeepers swap. The shots produced by the jet-ball are always varied as far as direction and time intervals are concerned but the power remains the same.	The goalkeepers do not control the situation. If they are correctly positioned they do not react to the shot from the jet-ball. If they save the shot their positioning is poor. They take too long to organize themselves and get back in position after the shot has been taken.
110	Multi-tasking. Concentration. Quick reflexes. Positioning. Coordination. Stretching and diving. Deflecting. Catching. Physical but especially mental effort.	22-32	3 goalkeepers. 2 act as 'flies' and the other in goal. They swap roles regularly. The 'jet-ball' machine is positioned 20 yards from goal. There is a mobile wall positioned 3 yards in front of each post. The 'jet-ball' can either shoot directly at goal or rebound the shot off either wall. The goalkeeper has to keep alert as he does not know when the shot is coming. The shots are very powerful and so the ball is often parried or 'spilled' and the goalkeeper has to deal with the 'flies'. The goalkeepers are swapped every two shots.	The goalkeeper is slow to react which is fatal. Lack of concentration. Not repositioning after saving the shot. The goalkeeper is so conscious of the walls that sometimes goals are scored down the middle.

No.	Objectives	Age	Developing the Games	Common Problems
111	Multi-tasking. Great concentration. Quick reflexes. Stretching and diving. Catching. Deflecting. Physical but especially mental effort.	22-32	3 goalkeepers. 2 act as 'flies' and the other in goal. They swap roles regularly. The 'jet-ball' machine is positioned 20 yards from goal. There are no walls in this game. Instead, a sheet is placed along the line of the 6-yard box so that the goalkeeper cannot see the 'jet-ball' machine or the ball. The sheet takes the power out of the shot but it still reaches the goal. The goalkeeper has to react as soon as he sees where the ball is in order to save a goal being scored. The 'flies' are always nearby ready to score from any rebounds.	Lack of concentration. Lack of improvisation.
112	Multi-tasking. Great concentration. Focused and peripheral vision. Quick reflexes. Stretching and diving. Catching. Deflecting. Physical but especially mental effort.	22-32	Pitch size 40 x 30 yards. 2 goalkeepers take turns playing in each goal. 8 players run with a ball each from side to side of the central area of the pitch. Each player has been given a number from 1-8. 2 other players challenge for a ball. The coach calls out a number and the player shoots at either goal (if the goalkeeper is already in action in one goal he has to shoot at the other). The goalkeepers need to concentrate on all the players as they do not want to be taken by surprise.	Lack of concentration. Poor peripheral vision. Lack of improvisation. Not 'seeing' the shooter.

No.	Objectives	Age	Developing the Games	Common Problems
113	Multi-tasking. Great concentration. Focused and peripheral vision. Quick reflexes. Stretching and diving. Catching. Deflecting. Physical but especially mental effort.	22-32	3 goalkeepers alternate in goal. A jet-ball machine is placed in the corner of the pitch (later it is moved to the other corner). If the coach shouts 'one' the goalkeeper has to touch the right post, if he shouts 'two', the left post and if he shouts 'three' the goalkeeper jumps and touches the crossbar with both hands. When the coach shouts 'four' the goalkeeper touches the ground. When he hears the number 'five' the goalkeeper simulates a save (a catch, punching the ball away, a dive etc). The jet-ball launches a high ball at a reasonable pace into the penalty box at any time. The goalkeeper is concentrating on the numbers but at the same time he has to react and save the ball as it arrives. The goalkeeper needs to use a lot of imagination and improvisation as it does not matter how he saves the ball. The important thing is to save it (deflect it clear, jump to catch it, dive, punch with one or both hands etc). As soon as the save (or attempt) has been made the goalkeeper immediately gets back in position and responds to the numbers being shouted out by the coach. This is a very tiring game and so the goalkeepers swap regularly and take long rests in between.	Silly mistakes are made because of the extreme mental effort involved. Sometimes the goalkeeper does not even realize the ball is heading towards him. Lack of improvisation. This game needs to be repeated over many days so that the goalkeepers get accustomed to it.

No.	Objectives	Age	Developing the Games	Common Problems
114	Multi-tasking. Great concentration. Focused and peripheral vision. Quick reflexes. Stretching and diving. Catching. Deflecting. Tremendous physical and mental effort.	22-32	3 goalkeepers alternate in this game. There is a jet-ball machine in each corner. A group of players also alternate playing '1 v 1' on the edge of the 18-yard box to see who gets a chance to shoot at goal. The goalkeeper has to concentrate on both the balls by trying to save them or even stop the shot from being taken while also making sure that the jet-ball has not sent a ball in his direction. The ball delivered by the machine is always punched clear as quickly as possible. The goalkeepers swap roles frequently.	Sometimes the goalkeeper does not even realize the ball from the machine is heading towards him. If a player kicks the ball long in front of him the goalkeeper does not run out to claim the ball by diving on it. Poor anticipation. The goalkeeper does not guess which player is likely to win the '1 v 1' and come away with the ball.

No.	Objectives	Age	Developing the Games	Common Problems
115	Simulating real match situations. Multi-tasking: organizing the defense, coming off line, stretching and diving, anticipation, catching, releasing the ball with hands and feet, punching etc).	22-32	1 goalkeeper in goal. 4 defenders (3 markers and a 'sweeper') and 3 attackers between the 6-yard box and the penalty spot. 2 more attackers are standing near the edge of the 18-yard box. There is a player with various balls on each wing (roughly in line with the 18-yard box). 2 other goalkeepers are jogging near the halfway line ready to receive the throw from the goalkeeper when he gets the ball. The players on the wing take turns going down the wing and crossing a high ball into the box on the run. The players in the box challenge for the ball in the air, head it, shoot and make clearances etc. The 2 attackers on the edge of the 18-yard box do not challenge for the ball, instead they wait to take advantage of the ball coming to them via a poor clearance or deflection. The move stops when a goal is scored, the ball goes out of play or the defenders pass the ball back to the goalkeeper. When the goalkeeper gets the ball he throws it out to the player in the best position to receive it near the halfway line (this also happens when the goalkeeper catches the ball from the cross or dives or saves it). The goalkeeper who receives the ball near the halfway line passes it to one of the players on the wing. The players swap roles frequently.	Generally the goalkeeper does not help to organize his defenders. Poor decision making when coming for crosses or staying put. The back passes to the goalkeeper are usually not good.

No.	Objectives	Age	Developing the Games	Common Problems
116	Simulating real match situations. Multi-tasking. Soaking up the pressure in the box.	22-32	This game basically involves a 'set play' where the main objective is playing as a unit and for the goalkeeper to catch the ball. There is a 'sweeper' but the marking is zonal. The defenders play the 'pressing' game and are therefore not in a line. When an attacker has the ball on the wing the full back and midfield player on that side of the pitch do the 'pressing'. Depending on the location of the ball all the defenders could be involved directly or indirectly in the 'pressing'. From time to time the coach may intervene and give the ball back to the attacking team so that they can build an attack from a different area. It is up to the goalkeeper to organize his defense.	In this type of game the goalkeeper shouts instructions a lot but rarely gets involved in the action. He usually likes the reverse to be true. The goalkeeper intervenes as if he was playing as the 'sweeper' even though one of his teammates has been given this role.

No.	Objectives	Age	Developing the Games	Common Problems
117	Perfecting defensive play. Playing with discipline and organization. Concentration. Multi-tasking. Tactical play.	22-32	Pitch size half the pitch. This game involves preparing the defense for the next match. A goalkeeper, 4 defenders and 2 midfield players take on 7 attackers. The latter play in a similar way to the next opponent. The defenders use zonal marking, cover, interchange positions and most importantly play as a well-organized unit. If the defenders win possession of the ball they pass it back to the goalkeeper who kicks it long to the other goalkeeper jogging along the halfway line (waiting for his turn to play). He then passes the ball back to the attackers and the game starts again. It is up to the goalkeeper to organize the defenders.	The goalkeeper does not help to organize the defense. He does not shout instructions to the players 'day-dreaming' (and there is always one). Once the defenders win the ball they do not play it back to the goalkeeper so that he can kick it long.

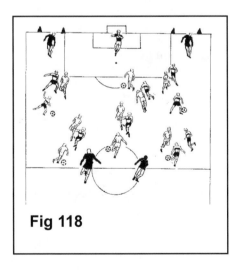

Fig 118

No.	Objectives	Age	Developing the Games	Common Problems
118	Spatial awareness. Focused and peripheral vision. Multi-tasking. Concentration. Quick reflexes. Dealing with close and long distance shots. Mastering the '1 v 1'.	22-32	Pitch size half the pitch. 3 goals are used, the regulation size goal and 2 other goals near the corners of the pitch. There are 5 goalkeepers, 1 in each goal and 2 on the halfway line (of the regulation size pitch) waiting to receive the long pass and take a turn to play. 18 players are split into groups of 3 (1 ball per group) where a '2v1' situation is created. The player on the ball is always harried and challenged by the other 2 players who employ the 'pressing' game. This player tries to keep possession and get close enough to one of the goals so that he can have a shot (the goalkeepers are passive). If one of the other two players wins the ball he is not allowed to shoot until he has overcome the 'pressing' game. In this case the goalkeepers monitor the situation and get ready to make an intervention. The player who wins the ball has to enter the area (the other 2 players are not allowed to follow him) and a '1 v 1' with the goalkeeper develops. The player is allowed to shoot or dribble. The goalkeepers also need to be aware of the 'jet-ball' machine that is strategically placed to launch powerful and accurate shots on any of the 3 goals at any time.	It is very difficult for the goalkeepers to concentrate on so many things at once. They react too late. They do not 'stand tall' and narrow the angle in the '1 v 1'. The players shoot before they overcome the 'pressing'. The player on the ball is followed into the area. This is not allowed.

No.	Objectives	Age	Developing the Games	Common Problems
119	Paying attention. Concentration. Spatial awareness. Coordination. Demonstrate improved mental and physical strength. Catching. Deflecting. Punching. Releasing the ball quickly and effectively.	22-32	The 'jet-ball' machine sends over accurate and powerful curling corners. A player stands as close as the rules allow to make sure that the ball has to be kicked high into the box. 1 player stands on the near post, 1 on the far post and another on the edge of the 18-yard box waiting to latch onto any rebound. There are 2 attackers on the edge of the area waiting for a rebound or a poor clearance and there are 3 others in the 6-yard box, generally getting in the goalkeeper's way. The goalkeeper has to try to overcome these difficulties by using jumping for the ball and catching it, deflecting it for a corner or punching it clear. The goalkeeper needs to be told (and needs to practice this) that if he is running for the ball and an attacker blocks his path then he should not stop but instead 'crash' into the player as the 'free-kick' will nearly always go in his favor. If the goalkeeper gets the ball he throws it out to one of the goalkeepers waiting his turn near the halfway line. The goalkeepers swap after facing 5-6 crosses.	The defenders take up poor positions (this is mainly the goalkeeper's fault). Indecision when thinking of the best way to deal with the cross. The goalkeeper stays in goal too long (even though this is not a physically demanding game it is mentally tiring and no goalkeeper has to work so hard and intensively during a match).

No.	Objectives	Age	Developing the Games	Common Problems
120	Paying attention. Concentration. Spatial awareness. Coordination. Demonstrating improved mental and physical strength. Catching. Deflecting. Punching. Releasing the ball quickly and effectively.	22-32	This game involves defending from throw-ins. The 4 defenders position themselves appropriately in the 18-yard box but never enter the 6-yard box which belongs exclusively to the goalkeeper. There are 3 attackers in the 6-yard box and 2 others on the edge of the 18-yard box waiting for any loose ball or rebound. The goalkeeper has to deal with the ball if it enters the 6-yard box. The 'jet-ball' machine 'fires' balls so that they dip when they get to the goal just as with the corners. The players are told what type of 'throw-in' to expect so that they can position themselves accordingly (the players are not warned once they become more experienced). As before the goalkeeper throws the ball out if he gets it and he rotates with his teammates.	Indecision when thinking of the best way to deal with the corner. The goalkeeper becomes nervous and stressed if he catches the ball surrounded by the attackers. He should relax and take a few steps to move away from them before he distributes the ball with a throw or a kick as he knows they are not allowed to impede him.

Fig 121

No.	Objectives	Age	Developing the Games	Common Problems
121	Concentration. Mastering the '1 v 1'. Anticipating the intentions of the opposition. Ability to react to different circumstances. Agility.	22-32	4 goalkeepers alternating in goal. 2 'walls' 8 yards apart are placed in between the 6-yard box and the penalty spot (sideways on to the goal). There are 4-5 players and various balls outside the 18-yard box. On the signal a player runs towards the goal with a ball. The goalkeeper comes off his line to narrow the angle. The '1 v 1 ' can end in the following ways: 1.The attacker shoots and the goalkeeper tries to save the ball. 2.The attacker tries to dribble round the goalkeeper (the latter dives to try to claim the ball). 3.The attacker chooses to shoot at goal by kicking the ball against one of the 'walls' (the goalkeeper 'reads' the move and dives in anticipation to save the ball or he scrambles back to try to get to the ball before it crosses the goal-line). 4.The attacker plays the 'one-two' by kicking the ball against either of the 'walls' (the goalkeeper reacts as in number 3). The game continues in this way with the goalkeepers swapping on a regular basis.	This is a very difficult game for the goalkeepers so it is better not to use the top strikers in order to give the former some confidence. Some goalkeepers 'give up' before the move has even started. These players will not do well in the sport.

No.	Objectives	Age	Developing the Games	Common Problems
122	Concentration. Physical and mental speed. Anticipating the intentions of the opposition. Feints and dummies. Not giving in.	22-32	Very similar to the previous game but only involving 1 'wall' which during the second half is moved to the other side. Another difference is that the attacker is supported by another player on the opposite side to the 'wall'. During the '1 v 1' the attacker can shoot or dribble. He is also able to pass to the other player but this is via a rebound off the 'wall'. He can obviously use feints and dummies to try to fool the goalkeeper. The goalkeeper can also (and should) employ these tactics and should try to anticipate the pass.	Passing the ball to the other player without using the 'wall'. This is not allowed. Faced by the goalkeeper, the player who received the ball decides to pass it back. This is not allowed. The goalkeeper moves across so far anticipating the pass that he leaves the goal exposed.
123	Concentration. Anticipating the intentions of the opposition. Learning to 'hold your ground' and wait. Positive attitude.	22-32	No 'walls' in this game, just continuous '1 v 1' situations. 3 attackers (1 on the right wing, 1 on the left and 1 in the middle) take turns running at goal. The goalkeeper has to come off his line to narrow the angle and be ready for a shot or dribble. These moves by the goalkeeper should be practiced after he has had a few goes at being the attacker and has gained some confidence about what to expect. The goalkeepers swap roles regularly.	The attacker is frustrated as he does not have as many things in his favor as in the previous games (the reverse is true for the goalkeeper). The goalkeeper does not try to provoke the attacker into making a mistake by playing feints and dummies.

No.	Objectives	Age	Developing the Games	Common Problems
124	Concentration. Quick reflexes. Ability to react to different circumstances. Agility. Spatial awareness.	22-32	This game uses 4 'walls'. 2 are positioned as in the previous games and the other 2 are on the 'dead-ball' line next to the posts. 1 goalkeeper in goal, a 'fly' and another 2 players some distance from these players and each other and either side. The 'jet-ball' machine is located 25 yards from the goal. The goalkeeper has to lay face-down on the goal-line. On the signal the goalkeeper stands up and turns, ready to face the ball that is launched from the 'jet-ball' directly at goal or to rebound into the goal off one of the 'walls' in the 18-yard box. The ball is sometimes rebounded off the 'walls' on the 'dead-ball' line so that it rebounds for the 'fly' to collect and score. If the goalkeeper is able to claim the ball he immediately throws it to the best-positioned goalkeeper jogging near the halfway line The goalkeepers swap roles on a regular basis.	At first the goalkeeper is not good at dealing with the rebounds but he quickly gets used to them. Sometimes a goalkeeper who is normally very positive 'freezes' once the 'fly' gets the ball from a rebound.

Fig 122

Fig 123

No.	Objectives	Age	Developing the Games	Common Problems
125	Paying attention. Concentration. Quick reflexes. Jumping. Heading. Long passes.	22-32	6 goalkeepers are put into pairs and these take turns in goal. The goalkeepers get themselves in position as the 'jet-ball' machine is located on the wing 10 yards from the corner. Suddenly a ball is launched into the penalty box and the 2 goalkeepers have to run out to try to head the ball. Sometimes the players misjudge the ball completely or their clearance is poor. After the attempt the players set off after the ball and the first to arrive controls it and passes it to one of the other goalkeepers waiting his turn. The other goalkeeper does his best to win the ball so that he is the one who makes the pass. Then the other pairings have a turn and the 'jet-ball' is later positioned on the other wing.	The goalkeepers are not of similar ability (they should always be as evenly matched as possible). Some goalkeepers do not bother to jump for the ball. Some fail to react after the header is made as they forget that they have to claim the ball and pass it.

No.	Objectives	Age	Developing the Games	Common Problems
126	Practicing the system. Concentration. Organizing the team. Heading.	22-32	Pitch size 35 x 20 yards. This is a '7-a-side' heading game. The players line up in the normal way and play 'the method'. The goalkeeper organizes the rest of the team. When he gets the ball he throws it up high and jumps to head it back in play. In order to make this game more physically demanding and to encourage diving, a goal is worth double if all the players (including the goalkeeper) are in the opposition's half when it is scored. A goal is worth 3 points if the above is true and one of the opposition is not in his own half. Penalties are always taken by the goalkeeper and they involve the following: the ball is kicked into the area and the goalkeeper performs a diving header.	The goalkeeper does not organize his teammates. Some forget to cross the halfway line when their team are attacking. The goalkeeper does not jump and head the ball to put it back in play.

Fig 126

No.	Objectives	Age	Developing the Games	Common Problems
127	Concentration. Focused and peripheral vision. Spatial awareness. Anticipation. Jumping. Heading.	22-32	This is a heading game. A goal is positioned 15 yards opposite the regulation size one. Apart from the goalkeepers, each team has 3 players who line up in a 'V' formation with each player being man-marked. The coach ensures that the players marking each other have the same heading ability. The players change roles (the attackers defend and the defenders attack) during the second half and the players make a note of how many goals they score. The game is played with 2 balls at the same time to improve concentration, anticipation and the number of headers taken. The coach throws another ball in towards one of the goals (without warning the players) as soon as one goes out of play.	Some defenders stop marking and decide to go on the attack (this must be stopped). A goal is scored with the second ball as the goalkeeper is in possession of the first one and looks around to see who to give it to. The goalkeeper needs to release the ball immediately. The players do not jump correctly (shoulder to shoulder) which could cause an injury.

No.	Objectives	Age	Developing the Games	Common Problems
128	Paying attention. Concentration. Quick reflexes. Performing confidently and assertively when faced by a series of simultaneous shots.	22-32	6 goalkeepers are put into 3 pairs and 12 outfield players are put into 3 groups of 4. 2 goalkeepers go in goal and 4 outfield players are positioned 30 yards away. Each of the players has 3 balls. The idea is for the players to shoot and score with all 3 balls and the goalkeepers have to try to save the shots. The shots have to be taken on the edge of the 18-yard box (never inside). The players can only run with 1 ball at a time and they only have a certain amount of time in which to try to score with all 3. So, they sprint to the edge of the box and shoot and then sprint back for another ball etc. When they have finished, 2 other goalkeepers go in goal and 4 new outfield players prepare to shoot. The quartet that scores the most goals (they have several attempts each) is the winner. The goalkeeper pairing who let in the least number of goals is the winner.	The 2 goalkeepers position themselves poorly and so do not 'fill' the goal. Some goalkeepers get in the other goalkeeper's way. The goalkeepers have to stay alert as the shots come thick and fast. Some players always shoot against the same goalkeepers. This should be avoided.

No.	Objectives	Age	Developing the Games	Common Problems
129	Concentration. Positioning. Spatial awareness (visual and abstract). Learning to 'hold your ground' and wait. Agility. Releasing the ball quickly and effectively.	22-32	6 players have a ball each. 4 cones form a square (3 x 3 yards) 10 yards away. This square is defended by a goalkeeper (2 others wait their turn). On the signal one of the players runs towards the square to try to score in any side. The goalkeeper constantly changes his position to cover either one of the four sides. If the goalkeeper gets the ball he kicks it to one of the other goalkeepers waiting to play. Another player then attacks the goal etc. The goalkeepers swap after facing 3 attacks. A note is made of how many goals each striker scores and how many saves the goalkeeper makes.	The goalkeeper sometimes dives before the striker shoots as he is fooled by the feints and dummies. The goalkeeper takes too long to dive at the player's feet because he does not lower his center of gravity.
130	Concentration. Positioning. Spatial awareness (visual and abstract). Agility. Moving quickly (explosive power). Releasing the ball quickly and effectively.	22-32	6 players have a ball each. 4 cones form a square (3 x 3 yards) 10 yards away. This square is defended by a goalkeeper (2 others wait their turn). In this game the players attack in pairs. They pass the ball to each other and try to score in any side of the square. A note is taken of how many goals each pair scores and how many times the goalkeeper saves the ball.	Poor positioning. Lack of speed. Some goalkeepers complain that the game is stopped just as they were 'warmed up'. The coach needs to explain that goalkeepers rarely perform in a match in this condition.

No.	Objectives	Age	Developing the Games	Common Problems
131	Concentration. Positioning. Focused and peripheral vision. Dealing with distractions. Playing in goal. Passing the ball quickly and effectively.	22-32	A goalkeeper in goal (2 others awaiting their turn) and a '2 v 2' taking place on the edge of the 18-yard box. 2 players are attacking and 2 are defending. There are 2 cones approximately 8 yards apart near the corners of the 18-yard box. 2 players run across the goal in and out of the cones. The goalkeeper concentrates on the '2 v 2' while the 2 players run across his line of vision. If the goalkeeper saves the ball he throws it out to one of the other goalkeepers waiting. All the players swap regularly.	Occasionally the players running across the goal get hit by the ball (they should use peripheral vision to avoid this). If an attacker gets into the 18-yard box the defenders do not give chase. The same is true of the players running around the cones. All the players should continue.

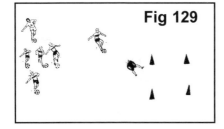

Fig 129

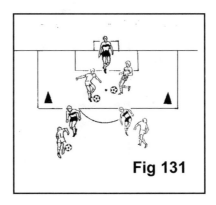

Fig 131

No.	Objectives	Age	Developing the Games	Common Problems
132	Paying attention. Concentration. Positioning. Focused and peripheral vision. Spatial awareness (visual and abstract). Playing in goal. Passing the ball quickly and effectively.	22-32	A goalkeeper in goal (2 others awaiting their turn) and a '2 v 2' taking place on the edge of the 18-yard box. 2 players are attacking and 2 are defending. There are 2 cones approximately 12 yards apart near the corners of the 18-yard box. 2 players run across the goal in and out of the cones. They shoot at goal once they have completed the figure eight around the 2 cones. The goalkeeper has to concentrate on both the '2 v 2' and the 2 players running across his line of vision. If the goalkeeper find himself trying to save too many shots at once he needs to show good will-power and determination and not give in. If the goalkeeper saves the ball he throws it out to one of the waiting goalkeepers. All the players swap regularly.	Occasionally the players running across the goal get hit by the ball (they should use peripheral vision to avoid this). If an attacker gets into the 18-yard box the defenders do not give chase. The same is true of the players running around the cones. All the players should continue. The 2 players running around the cones have similar ability (in this case it is best for one of the players to be better than the other so that the shots are not taken at the same time).

Fig 133

No.	Objectives	Age	Developing the Games	Common Problems
133	Paying attention. Concentration. Positioning. Anticipation. Mental effort and will-power. Playing in goal. Passing the ball quickly and effectively.	22-32	Another game with one goalkeeper in goal (2 others awaiting their turn). '2 v 2' with 2 'neutral' players who always help the attacking team. The game is 'one-touch'. The goalkeeper concentrates on the game and bases his decisions (change position or intervene etc) on what he sees. However, there is a slight problem: 3 of the coaching staff stand behind the goalkeeper and put him off by pulling his shirt, shouting at him, pinching him and holding onto him. The goalkeepers swap roles on a regular basis. The 'neutral' players also swap but not as frequently.	The goalkeeper loses concentration because he is concerned about the coaching staff. This means that his positioning is poor, he does not 'read' the game and fails to narrow the angle effectively.
134	Paying attention. Concentration. Positioning. Focused and peripheral vision. Spatial awareness (visual and abstract). Mobility and agility.	22-32	A goalkeeper (2 others await their turn) defends the 4 sides of a 2 x 2-yard square. 6 players surround the square in an attempt to cover all the available space. 2 balls are in use and the players are not allowed to shoot in a goal being defended by the goalkeeper. The goalkeeper concentrates on both the balls in the game and runs from goal to goal to prevent shots being taken. The goalkeepers swap on a regular basis.	The outfield players do not get themselves in a good position to shoot. The goalkeeper only concentrates on one ball and ignores the other one. It is also true that all the players get much better at this game after only a short time.

No.	Objectives	Age	Developing the Games	Common Problems
135	Multi-tasking. Concentration. Focused and peripheral vision. Spatial aware-ness (visual and abstract). Quick reflex-es. Releasing the ball quickly and effective-ly.	22-32	A 'round' formed by 6 players. The imaginary circle has a radius of approximately 18 yards. 2 goalkeepers are in the middle (2 others jog in the distance waiting to receive the ball from those inside). The players throw the ball to each other (short and long). At any time a player produces the 'scissor' kick or 'half scissor' kick, aiming the ball towards the 2 goal-keepers in the middle. The goalkeepers concen-trate on both the balls in the game trying to save them. If a goalkeeper gets the ball he immediately throws it to one of the goalkeepers jogging in the distance. The goalkeepers swap regularly. A note is taken of the number of times each goalkeeper distributes the ball.	Some goalkeepers are ready to save all the shots whereas other see very few coming. Some goalkeepers wait for the ball to come to them whereas others anticipate and claim more balls. The 'scissor' kick tech-nique is difficult. Players should practice this skill if they have difficulty with it.
136	Quick reflex-es. Mental agility. Anticipation.	22-32	3 pairs take turns playing this game. The 2 players stand near the penalty spot with 4 balls 6 yards away: 1 in front of them, 1 behind them, 1 to their right and 1 to their left. On the coach's signal the players set off and try to claim the specified ball. However, if the coach calls out 'front' they have to get the ball behind and if he shouts 'left' they run right etc. When the goal-keeper claims a ball he immediately throws it out to one of the other goal-keepers. The players swap on a regular basis.	The goalkeepers are not evenly matched. Not running towards the specified ball. Not moving when the signal is made (the mind goes blank).

No.	Objectives	Age	Developing the Games	Common Problems
137	Making space. Long and short passes. Changing the game. 'Reading' the game. Playing as an outfield player (in a specific area and all over the pitch)	22-25	A game involving 8 players. Pitch size goes from the edge of one 18-yard box to the other. There are 3 goals (no goalkeepers) on each 18-yard box 3 yards wide marked by cones. A goalkeeper playing in the center circle has the job of organizing the play. The outfield players have no restrictions but the game involves man-to-man marking. They attack the 6 goals and any player can run with the ball between the cones to score 2 points. The players also combine with the goalkeeper in the center circle (no one else can enter this area). Every move involving the goalkeeper is worth 1 point. If the goalkeeper receives the ball halfway through the build-up then he has to change the direction or impetus of the play. If the other team wins possession they have to pass to the goalkeeper so that he can begin the attacking move. The rest of the goalkeepers in the squad play as outfield players until it is their turn to play in the center circle.	Not making space in the center circle in order to facilitate the moves. The opposition enter the center circle to try to win the ball. This is not allowed. The players do not involve the goalkeeper in the play. This means they lose points and the main objective of the game is lost: the goalkeepers improve using their feet and their 'soccer brain'.

Fig 136

No.	Objectives	Age	Developing the Games	Common Problems
138	Making space. Long and short passes. Keeping possession. Changing the game. Varying the pace of the game ('slowing' the game down). Playing in goal. Quick reflexes. Focused and peripheral vision.	22-25	A game involving 8 players. Pitch size goes from the edge of one 18-yard box to the other. There are 4 small goals (no goalkeepers) 2 on each 18-yard box. A goalkeeper plays in a regulation size goal on the halfway line. One team attacks the 5 goals (goals can be scored from either side of the goal on the halfway line) while the other team just try to keep possession if they win it by using the goalkeeper to help achieve this objective. After the signal from the coach the teams swap roles. The team who scores the most goals and keeps possession the longest wins (however the team who scores the most goals is not always the team who keeps possession the longest).	The players are not allowed to enter the center circle either to shoot or get the ball off the goalkeeper. The team trying to keep possession does not make use of the goalkeeper to gain a numerical advantage. The team in possession does not 'slow' the game down.

No.	Objectives	Age	Developing the Games	Common Problems
139	Paying attention. Concentration. Getting used to the size of the goal. Organizing the defense. The ability to judge 'time' (all the players). The coach gets a better understanding of the goalkeeper's limitations.	22-25	Pitch size goes from the edge of one 18-yard box to the other. There is a goal at both ends measuring 10 x 3 yards. The game is '9 a-side' with a 3-3-2 formation playing the moves in 'the method'. The idea is to produce as many shots on goal as possible. The game is played with these rules: 1.The goals are so big to encourage shots from distance. 2.The team in possession has 15 seconds to shoot. 3.If this does not happen the opposition takes a penalty from the halfway line. 4.If a team has not shot and time is running out then the goalkeeper organizes the team to play the 'pressing' game. The goalkeeper needs to concentrate on all aspects of the play and is expected not only to guard his goal but also to play away from it when the circumstances dictate.	Few long shots are practiced. Inability to judge the 15 seconds correctly (teams either go beyond it or shoot too quickly thinking it is about to expire). Inexperienced goalkeepers should not play with these huge goals on a regular basis as their spatial awareness suffers when playing in a normal sized goal. (it is very beneficial for experienced goalkeepers to play this game)

Fig 139

194

No.	Objectives	Age	Developing the Games	Common Problems
140	Paying attention. Concentration. Organizing the rest of the team. The ability to judge 'time' (all the players). Dealing with long shots. Positioning.	22-25	Pitch size 80 x 30 yards. 16 players (4 teams of 4). 2 teams play against each other and every 5 minutes another 2 teams take part. The game is played with these rules: 1.A line is drawn 25 yards on each side of the pitch so that the play takes place in the 30 yards in the middle. 2.The team in possession has to shoot in 10 seconds. 3.If this does not happen they concede a penalty (taken from the 25-yard line). 4.Shots can only be taken in the 30-yard area. 5.If a player shoots from within the 25 yard area a penalty is awarded. 6.The goalkeeper is expected to play in goal and also organize his teammates. A note is taken of all the goals scored and how many goals each individual goalkeeper concedes.	Poor positioning by the goalkeeper (he is usually too far off his line). Poor distribution of the ball (sometimes because the outfield players do not make space). Not judging the time effectively.

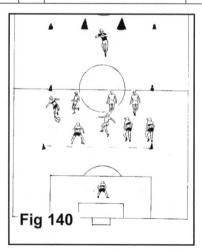

Fig 140

No.	Objectives	Age	Developing the Games	Common Problems
141	Multi-tasking. Concentration. Focused and peripheral vision. Quick reflexes. Dominating the space around you (visual and abstract). Positioning. Dealing with long shots. The ability to judge 'time' (all the players).	22-25	This is an identical game to the previous one. The only difference is that both teams play at the same time (i.e. two matches are played simultaneously). The number of players in the limited space makes it very difficult to play this game. The goalkeeper is kept very busy as there is only one in each game. He has to concentrate on both games and he has poor visibility because of the number of bodies in the way. The goalkeepers are swapped on a regular basis. The goalkeeper never goes to retrieve a ball that goes wide of the goal (the coach throws another ball on). If a penalty is awarded the goalkeeper has to try to save it while keeping an eye on the other game that is still in progress. A note is taken of all the goals scored and how many goals each individual goalkeeper concedes.	Poor positioning by the goalkeeper (he is usually too far off his line). Inability to concentrate on both games at once (lack of peripheral vision or ability to 'read' the game).

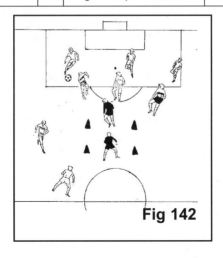

Fig 142

No.	Objectives	Age	Developing the Games	Common Problems
142	Paying attention. Concentration. Quick reflexes. Positioning. Anticipation. Playing in goal. Releasing the ball quickly.	22-32	Pitch size 50 x 30 yards. There are two regulation size goals 3 yards apart (one behind the other) in the middle of the pitch. There is a goalkeeper in each goal. The game is played '4 v 4' with the teams trying to score in both goals (there are no nets so the ball can enter the first goal and then the second). If the ball rebounds off a goalkeeper an attacker can shoot again. If a goalkeeper deflects a ball then a defender has to combine with the goalkeeper and shoot from the other side of the pitch. If the goalkeeper claims a ball then he immediately throws it to the other team so that they can mount an attack, move onto the other side of the pitch and shoot. The team who scores the most goals wins.	Lack of concentration. Poor passes (passing to the other team or to the team that has just shot) The defending team either gets the ball given to them by the goalkeeper or they win it, either way they should not shoot until they have moved onto the other side of the pitch.

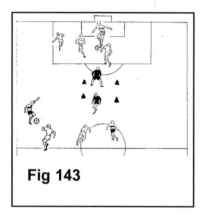

Fig 143

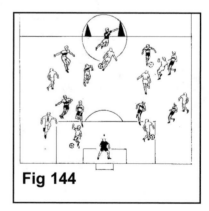

Fig 144

No.	Objectives	Age	Developing the Games	Common Problems
143	Multi-tasking. Concentration. Quick reflexes. Focused and peripheral vision. Dominating the space around you (visual and abstract). Playing in goal. Positioning. Releasing the ball quickly.	24-30	Pitch size 50 x 30 yards. There are two regulation size goals 3 yards apart (one behind the other) in the middle of the pitch. There is a goalkeeper in each goal and two more waiting to swap in. 8 players playing 2 simultaneous games of '2 v 2'. Just as in the previous game shots can be taken from both sides. If the ball is won the ball has to be taken to the other side of the pitch before a shot can be taken. If a goalkeeper gathers the ball he passes it to one of the goalkeepers waiting to play who in turn passes it to the other team.	Inability to concentrate on both games at once (lack of peripheral vision or ability to 'read' the game). Getting out of position (this is normal but the player must know how to re-position quickly and effectively). Forgetting to save the ball in both the goals.
144	Multi-tasking. Concentration. Quick reflexes. Focused and peripheral vision. Dominating the space around you (visual and abstract). Playing in goal. Positioning.	24-30	Pitch size 40 x 40 yards. 2 regulation size goals with a goalkeeper in each. 4 games of '2 v 2' played simultaneously involving 8 teams of 2 outfield players. The goalkeepers have to concentrate on all 4 balls. The game is 'one-touch' (max 'two-touch'). If a goal is scored or a shot goes wide the goalkeepers have to continue to concentrate on the other balls in play. If they claim a ball they immediately throw it back in play and do the same. All the players in the game swap after 5 minutes because the game is very tiring. A note is taken of how many goals each goalkeeper concedes.	It is very difficult to concentrate on all four games at once. It is very difficult to get in the correct position. (both these aspects need to be worked on).

No.	Objectives	Age	Developing the Games	Common Problems
145	Paying attention. Concentration. Quick reflexes. Dominating the space around you. Positioning. Playing in goal. Releasing the ball quickly and effectively.	22-32	Pitch size half the pitch. '7 v 7'. The goals are formed by 3 cones 6 yards apart forming a triangle. In reality this makes 3 goals on either side to aim at and the goalkeepers need to cover all 3, which is very difficult. The defenders also have a difficult job as they are organized and controlled by the goalkeepers.	Poor positioning by the goalkeeper. The goalkeeper does not organize the defenders effectively.
146	Perfecting the 'off-side' trap. The role of the goalkeeper in the above tactic. Organizing the rest of the team. Concentration. Analyzing the game. Anticipation. Playing as an outfield player.	22-32	'11 v 11' practice match is played on a regulation size pitch. The defenders push up and play the 'pressing' game. The player on the ball is not given time or space. The goalkeeper is familiar with the tricks and tactics the opposition will employ to try to beat the 'off-side' trap: 1.Playing the 'one-two' with a striker and then running onto the pass which is played behind the defenders. 2.Playing a pass behind the defenders into the path of a runner who comes from a deep position. 3.Playing an individual move (dribbling or the 'auto-pass' etc). The goalkeeper plays off his line and needs to intercept balls beyond his 18-yard box if his defenders are beaten.	Some goalkeepers do not move far forwards fearing a long shot will go over their head (the player on the ball needs to be under constant pressure so that he does not have the time or space to shoot). No instructions given to the rest of the team. The goalkeeper reaches the ball but he 'shows off' and gets into difficulty (The ball should be kicked out if in doubt as this gives the team a chance to regroup and reorganize).

No.	Objectives	Age	Developing the Games	Common Problems
147	Adapting to playing in a specific area. Organizing the rest of the team. Forming the wall quickly and effectively. Anticipation in the 18-yard box.	22-32	'11 v 11' practice match is played on a regulation size pitch (the smallest the rules allow). This simulates the pitch-size they will encounter during the next match. The 'first-team' play the same way as they expect the opposition to play. The limited space means that the ball reaches the 18-yard box more often either through passes or 'throw-ins' and there are more dangerous 'free-kicks' requiring an effective 'wall'. The goalkeeper has to cope with all these problems. The coach asks the players to repeat any move that is not played properly.	The goalkeeper does not organize his team-mates at corners or 'throw-ins'. The players take too long to form the wall. Poor anticipation in the 18-yard box.

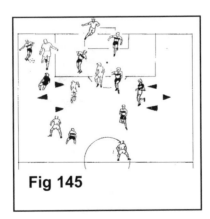

Fig 145

No.	Objectives	Age	Developing the Games	Common Problems
148	Paying attention. Concentration. Psychological work. Organizing the defense. The goalkeeper needs to know the playing system and 'game plan'.	22-32	Using half the pitch. A goalkeeper, 3 defenders and 3 midfield players take on 8 attackers playing the moves in 'the method'. If the defenders get the ball they try to 'slow' the game down by keeping possession and not taking any risks. If they can do nothing with the ball it is played to the coach who gives it to the opposition so that they can mount another attack. The following is done to make the game more competitive and intense: The coach shouts out that there are 5 minutes remaining and that the defenders are winning 1-0. If the attackers draw level the defenders still win the game and so the former have to score at least 2 goals to win. If the necessary goals are not scored the coach plays another 5 minutes of 'extra time'.	The pressure on the attackers to win the game is a great motivational factor but at times they forget to play the moves in 'the method'. The goalkeeper does not organize the rest of his teammates.

No.	Objectives	Age	Developing the Games	Common Problems
149	Improving the other senses. Improving perception. Ability to 'sense' things that they would not have been able to capture before. Dealing with situations that would have been problematic in the past.	22-32	2 goalkeepers (one wearing a blindfold) are running backwards and forwards across the 18-yard box. The sighted player tells the other player every time they run past the goal. This is repeated and the idea is to increase the perception and awareness of the player wearing the blindfold. During training sessions when blindfolds are used the player runs alone and has to 'sense' when he is passing the goal (always bear in mind that no 2 players will do these exercises exactly the same).	At first, for his own safety, the goalkeeper should run with one arm out in front of him and the other across his chest. The goalkeeper is too worried about bumping into someone or something, which means he is not aware of what is going on around him.
150	Paying attention. Concentration. Orientation. Spatial awareness. Dominating the space (abstract).	22-32	The goalkeeper makes a mental note of what he sees in the 18-yard box: a ball on the penalty spot, a teammate in goal and 2 attackers out wide. He is located just outside the 18-yard box. He puts on a blindfold and with his arms stretched out in front of him he moves, names and touches all that he has seen. As he gets better he only uses one arm in front of him and he jogs to each position.	Some goalkeepers have a very poor sense of direction (this is a particularly good exercise for them). Not stretching the arms out in front. Lack of concentration.

Fig 150

No.	Objectives	Age	Developing the Games	Common Problems
151	Controlling and manipulating the time. Judging different lengths of time. Concentration.	22-32	5 goalkeepers wearing blindfolds have to estimate and judge how much time has passed (just as in games). They indicate by raising their arm when they think 5, 10, 14, 21 and 30 seconds is up. At first the time is never-ending or it is over in an instant. However, the players all develop this skill and make considerable progress as it is repeated over the weeks.	Some start off well but soon deteriorate. Those who start off badly get worse and worse. Some goalkeepers lose concentration completely (this is only at first).
152	Coordination. Moving sideways. A good 'feel' for the ball. Concentration.	22-32	3 goalkeepers, all wearing blindfolds control and manipulate the ball (both stationary and on the move). First the goalkeeper bounces the ball with his stronger hand and then with the weaker one. Next he bounces the ball using both hands. Once this is mastered the goalkeeper walks and goes through the same routine. Finally he moves onto jogging slowly.	This control is so difficult that it is very important that the goalkeeper does not move onto the next stage before fully mastering the previous one.

Fig 152

Fig 153

Fig 154

No.	Objectives	Age	Developing the Games	Common Problems
153	Concentration. Coordination. A good 'feel' for the ball.	22-32	Very similar to the previous game but a lot more difficult. 2 cones are positioned 5 yards apart. The goalkeeper has the ball in his hands as he has a good look at the obstacle course he has to complete once he puts on the blindfold. Once he is unsighted he bounces the ball around the cones in a figure eight and returns to the starting position. Then the next player does the same. Once this is mastered, the next task is to do the same going backwards.	This control is so difficult that it is very important that the goalkeeper does not move onto the next stage before fully mastering the previous one.
154	Paying attention. Concentration. Orientation. Dominating the space around you (abstract). Improving auditory sense. Performing at speed.	22-32	A goalkeeper stands in goal observing the coach who is on the penalty spot holding a ball. When he is ready he asks for the blindfold and prepares to save the ball. The coach makes sure the ball bounces hard before it reaches the goalkeeper. The goalkeeper listens for the bounce and at the very least tries to save the ball and at best gather it (ideally he does both). Before trying again the goalkeeper removes the blindfold and the coach outlines any mistakes he made so that he can correct them during the next attempt. The coach also points out anything the goalkeeper did well as this is a great motivational factor.	Lack of concentration. Some goalkeepers can stop the ball but they are unable to claim it even though it is very close to them (this shows a lack of abstract spatial awareness). Some coaches forget to tell the goalkeeper about all the good things he does.

204

No.	Objectives	Age	Developing the Games	Common Problems
155	Paying attention. Concentration. Orientation. Dominating the space around (abstract). Improving auditory sense. Throwing the ball out effectively. Performing the technique automatically.	22-32	4 goalkeepers. 1 in goal with a ball and the other 3 lined up across the pitch 30 yards away. The goalkeeper in the goal has a good look to see where these players are standing before putting on a blindfold. The other 3 players are then allowed to move a maximum of 3 yards (forwards, backwards left or right). On the signal one of the players calls for the ball and the goalkeeper throws the ball to him, basing the distance and direction on where he remembers the player being and where the noise is coming from. Positive constructive criticism is made on the throws. All the goalkeepers have a turn in goal.	Some goalkeepers find it difficult to bend down to pick the ball up. Poor passes (due to lack of spatial memory, not locating the sound or both.
156	Paying attention. Concentration. Orientation. Improving auditory sense. Positioning.	22-32	A goalkeeper in goal wearing a blindfold. 3 others spread out in the 18-yard box with a ball each. One of the players shouts and the goalkeeper advances towards the sound and stops where he thinks he is best positioned to narrow the angle. The coach places a cone to mark the spot. Then the other 2 players take turns shouting out and the same thing happens. The coach then discusses the position of the cones with the goalkeeper.	Poor positioning. The goalkeeper either comes too far forwards or stays too far back.

No.	Objectives	Age	Developing the Games	Common Problems
157	Paying attention. Concentration. Spatial awareness. Dominating the space around you (abstract). Improving auditory sense. Performing at speed.	22-32	2 goalkeepers, both wearing blindfolds, play this game at the same time. 1 stands in goal and the other (playing as the attacker) on the edge of the 18-yard box. The coach asks if they are ready and then bounces the ball near the penalty spot. The players move forwards trying to claim the ball once they hear the bounce. If the attacker touches the ball he tells the goalkeeper but continues on to try to score. The goalkeeper does his best to stop a goal being scored. The players swap roles.	Poor spatial awareness. This game is particularly good for any players with poor hearing.
158	Paying attention. Concentration. Balance. Getting a 'feel' for the ball. Doing this automatically.	22-32	2 goalkeepers take turns playing this game. One of them is wearing a blindfold and is 8 yards from a basketball hoop (the other player tells him how he is doing). Then the players swap roles. The player who scores the most baskets is the winner.	Poor balance. Not producing the correct throwing technique. The players do not use their sense, master the technique and then get into a rhythm (this is what the exercise is about).

Fig 157

No.	Objectives	Age	Developing the Games	Common Problems
159	Orientation. Balance. Coordination.	22-32	A goalkeeper in goal holding a ball, another in line with one post 10 yards away and a third in line with the other post 10 yards away. The latter sets off towards the goal while the goalkeeper throws the ball to him. He does a forward roll and then throws himself at the ball either catching it or deflecting it towards the other goalkeeper. He immediately gets up, does another forward roll and heads for the goalkeeper who throws out another ball for him to head at goal. Then the goalkeepers swap roles. A note is taken of good technique and goals scored.	Poor coordination. Poor balance. The diving header after the forward roll makes some goalkeepers feel sick.
160	Balance. Coordination. Adaptability.	22-32	Various goalkeepers alternate in this game: 1 gets on a wooden cylinder holding a ball. He does as many different ball-skills as he can while he keeps his balance on the wooden cylinder. The exercise is brief but is repeated often.	Some goalkeepers find it very difficult to keep their balance on the wooden cylinder (they should concentrate on this and not try any ball-skills). Some try extremely complicated tricks. The players should start off by performing simple ball-skills and progress onto more difficult ones.

Other Books by Laureano Ruiz Available from Reedswain

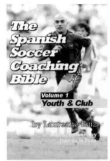

The Spanish Soccer Coaching Bible
Volume 1
Youth and Club

The Spanish Soccer Coaching Bible
Volume 2
High School and College

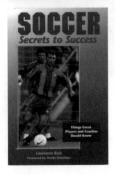

Soccer: Secrets to Success
Things Great Players and Coaches Should
Know

visit us at www.reedswain.com
or
call toll free at 800-331-5191

Also available from Reedswain:

#185 **Conditioning for Soccer**
by Raymond Verheijen
$19.95

#188 **300 Innovative Soccer Drills**
by Roger Wilkinson and Mick Critchell
$14.95

#290 **Practice Plans for Effective
     Training**
by Ken Sherry
$14.95

#787 **Attacking Schemes and
     Training Exercises**
by Eugenio Fascetti and Romedio Scaia
$14.95

#788 **Zone Play**
by Angelo Pereni and Michele di Cesare
$14.95

#792 **120 Competitive Games and
     Exercises**
by Nicola Pica
$14.95

#793 **Coaching the 5-3-2**
by Eugenio Fascetti and Romedio Scaia
$14.95

www.reedswain.com
800.331.5191

Also available from Reedswain: